# The Summer Island Site

# THE SUMMER ISLAND SITE

*A Study of Prehistoric Cultural Ecology and Social Organization in the Northern Lake Michigan Area*

## DAVID S. BROSE

NUMBER 1

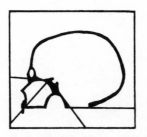

CASE WESTERN RESERVE UNIVERSITY
STUDIES IN ANTHROPOLOGY

Case Western Reserve University
Studies in Anthropology
James E. Fitting, *Series Editor*

No. 1. The Summer Island Site: A Study of Prehistoric Cultural Ecology and Social Organization in the Northern Lake Michigan Area. *By David S. Brose.* 1970.

No. 2. Metric Trends in Hominid Dental Evolution. *By Milford H. Wolpoff.* Forthcoming.

No. 3. Life-Crisis Rituals Among the Kenuz. *By Charles Callender and Fadwa el Guindi.* Forthcoming.

International Standard Book Number: 0-8295-0187-8.

Library of Congress Catalogue Card Number: 70-84486.

# *Preface*

The present work represents an attempt to interpret some of the less obvious aspects of the prehistory of the Northern Great Lakes area. The key to the interpretations offered herein was provided by the excavation and analyses of the Summer Island site. Much of this work was supported by the National Science Foundation Grant (GS-1486), "Archaeological Investigations in Michigan," awarded to Dr. James E. Fitting, then the the University of Michigan. The work of previous Great Lakes archaeologists was indispensable in the formulation of many of the hypotheses formulated in the course of this project. Chief among these were George Quimby, Warren Wittry, James Fitting, Ronald Mason, James Wright, and Alan McPherron. In a wider context, the work of James Brown, Charles Cleland, James Deetz, Leslie Freeman, James Griffin, Robert Hall, William Longacre, William Ritchie, James Stoltman, and Robert Whallon, has contributed greatly to the framework in which these archaeological investigations must be understood, and in the methods of analysis which could be applied.

This paper represents a portion of a considerably larger work, *The Archaeology of Summer Island: Changing Settlement Systems in Northern Lake Michigan,* which comprised my dissertation submitted in partial fulfillment of the requirements for the degree of Doctor of Philosophy in The University of Michigan, 1968. I have expressed my appreciation to the members of my committee, James Fitting, James Griffin, Volney Jones, Robert Warner, and Aram Yengoyan of The University of Michigan for reading and commenting upon earlier versions of this paper. My colleagues at Case Western Reserve University, Leo A. Despres and Charles Callender, have also read and commented upon this portion of the report, for which I am quite grateful. Needless to say, the conclusions arrived at are my responsibility, often in defiance of these most helpful critics.

I should also like to express my thanks to Mr. Terry Brooks and Mr. Dan Stevens, of Summer Science Inc., for their encouragement and logistic support during the six weeks spent in excavations on Summer Island. Mrs. Millie Smith typed and corrected the final manuscript version of this paper, for which I acknowledge considerable debt.

Last, but certainly far from least, were the efforts of my wife, Barbara, who helped in the analysis and cataloging of artifacts and in their photography. She also composed the photographic plates, collated and ordered tables and figures, read, edited, and corrected the final version of the manuscript, and provided moral encouragement throughout the ordeal.

# *Contents*

**1.** Introduction . . . . . . . . . . . . . . . . . . . . . . . . . . . . . . . . . . . . . . . . . . . . . . . . . . . . 3

**2.** Environment . . . . . . . . . . . . . . . . . . . . . . . . . . . . . . . . . . . . . . . . . . . . . . . . . . 5

**3.** Archaeological Excavations . . . . . . . . . . . . . . . . . . . . . . . . . . . . . . . . . 12

**4.** The Middle Woodland Component: Material Culture . . . . . . . . . . . . . . . 14

**5.** Economy . . . . . . . . . . . . . . . . . . . . . . . . . . . . . . . . . . . . . . . . . . . . . . . . . . . 28

**6.** Middle Woodland Features and Structures . . . . . . . . . . . . . . . . . . . . . . 31

**7.** Areal Distributions . . . . . . . . . . . . . . . . . . . . . . . . . . . . . . . . . . . . . . . . . . 44

**8.** Conclusions . . . . . . . . . . . . . . . . . . . . . . . . . . . . . . . . . . . . . . . . . . . . . . . . 66

References . . . . . . . . . . . . . . . . . . . . . . . . . . . . . . . . . . . . . . . . . . . . . . . . 69

# List of Tables

I. Climate of Summer Island Area . . . . . . . . . . . . . . . . . . . . . . . . . . . . . 11
II. Distribution of Post-Mold Diameters . . . . . . . . . . . . . . . . . . . . . . . . . 20
III. Middle Woodland Post-Mold Size Against Location . . . . . . . . . . . . . . . . . 20
IV. Ceramics from Middle Woodland Component . . . . . . . . . . . . . . . . . . . . 22
V. Middle Woodland Ceramic by Percent of Vessel from Component . . . . . . . . 23
VI. Middle Woodland Ceramic Taxonomy . . . . . . . . . . . . . . . . . . . . . . . . 25
VII. Chipped-Stone Material from 134 Middle Woodland Excavation Units . . . . . 26
VIII. Identifiable Faunal Remains from Middle Woodland Component . . . . . . . . . 29
IX. Middle Woodland Features . . . . . . . . . . . . . . . . . . . . . . . . . . . . . . . 32
X. Mean Rim Diameters for Middle Woodland Vessels . . . . . . . . . . . . . . . . 46
XI. Correlation Coefficient Matrix: Middle Woodland Ceramics . . . . . . . . . . . 50
XII. Correlation Coefficient Matrix: Middle Woodland Bone and Stone . . . . . . . . 61

# List of Figures

1. Map 1: Northern Lake Michigan . . . . . . . . . . . . . . . . . . . . . . . . . . . . . 6
2. Map 2: Southern Delta County, Michigan . . . . . . . . . . . . . . . . . . . . . . . 8
3. Map 3: The Summer Island Site . . . . . . . . . . . . . . . . . . . . . . . . . . . . . 9
4. Middle Woodland Occupation in Area "C" . . . . . . . . . . . . . . . . . . . . . . 17
5. North-South Stratigraphic Profile . . . . . . . . . . . . . . . . . . . . . . . . . . . 18
6. East-West Stratigraphic Profile . . . . . . . . . . . . . . . . . . . . . . . . . . . . 19
7. Reconstruction of Ground Plan of Community . . . . . . . . . . . . . . . . . . . . 20
8. Distribution of Material on Floors . . . . . . . . . . . . . . . . . . . . . . . . . . . 41
9. Mean Sherd Weight by Provenience Unit . . . . . . . . . . . . . . . . . . . . . . . 48
10. Schematic Representation of Ceramic Clusters at Structural Locii . . . . . . . . . 56
11. Schematic Representation of Ceramic Design Transmission with Patrilateral
    Cross-Cousin Marriage and Patrilocality . . . . . . . . . . . . . . . . . . . . . . . 57

# List of Plates

I. Summer Island from the North (Point Detour) . . . . . . . . . . . . . . . . . . . . . . 7
II. Two Views of the Summer Island Site . . . . . . . . . . . . . . . . . . . . . . . . 15
III. Midden Floors and Post-Molds from Middle Woodland Component . . . . . . . . 16
IV. Varieties of Middle Woodland Ceramics from Summer Island . . . . . . . . . . . . 24
V. Reconstructed Vessel from the Middle Woodland Component of Summer Island. . 47

# The Summer Island Site

# 1. Introduction

Within the upper Great Lakes region the northern Lake Michigan basin has received the greatest amount of recent archaeological attention. In northeastern Wisconsin, Mason (1966, 1967) has excavated and reported three sites which clearly demonstrate the chronological sequence from Middle Woodland through early Late Woodland to the final Upper Mississippian. His Middle Woodland North Bay culture at the Mero and the Ports des Morts sites was seen to be related to late Illinois Hopewellian cultures as well as to the more northern Laurel-Saugeen-Point Peninsula complexes. The early Late Woodland occupations at the Mero and Heins Creek sites were closely related to developments in eastern Wisconsin and northern Michigan. The Oneota component at the Mero site was related to developments in eastern Wisconsin whose chronological placement was somewhat uncertain.

On Bois Blanc Island, McPherron (1967) excavated the Juntunen site which demonstrated the Late Woodland chronological sequence in the region of Mackinac Straits. In the earliest Mackinac phase these were seen to be closely related to the Heins Creek complex in Wisconsin, while later phases seemed oriented to developments to the east.

Binford and Quimby (1963) analyzed the lithic industries from several sites in the northern Lake Michigan area and came to the conclusion that a rather specialized bipolar core technique was characteristic of the Late Woodland period (idem:306).

Fitting (1968) analyzed several sites from the Garden Peninsula and concluded that within this region many of the differences displayed by the lithic industry were a function of site utilization as much as of chronological placement.

The investigation of several sites along the north shore of Lake Michigan (Fitting, 1968b; Janzen, 1968; Cleland and Peske, 1968; Brose, 1968; Prahl and Brose, n.d.) clearly revealed that at any period of time several different types of sites could be found within this area. Many of the differences between these sites were clearly due to differing functions, and Fitting (idem) was able to interpret these as an indication that the economic adaptation in this area produced seasonally occupied sites with distinct characteristics.

In attempting a synthesis of these data it became clear that several crucial pieces of information were lacking. No major settlement attributable to the Middle Woodland period had been analyzed, hampering any reconstruction of the economic adaptation. The precise cultural relationships between the North Bay culture and the Laurel occupations to the north were poorly understood, and no acceptable processual explanation for their chronological placement or ceramic similarity was available. Nor was any explanation available for the apparent lithic similarities in the Late Woodland period in this area.

Several archaeological surveys indicated the possibility of the large, well-stratified site on Summer Island which contained Middle Woodland, Oneota, and Late Woodland components. The excavation of the site and the subsequent analysis of materials were undertaken by the

3

author from July 1967 to June 1968. It was hoped that these analyses would provide answers to some questions regarding the nature of adaptation to the agriculturally marginal environment of northern Lake Michigan as well as aiding in the solution of other problems.

In this paper the metric and morphological analysis of the material culture is not present. Those data have already been published elsewhere (Brose, n.d.b). Here, attention is given to the cultural ecology of the archaeological community. The topography and geomorphology of the area is discussed, and an analysis of the biotic and cultural environment is presented. The detailed analysis of the distribution and signifi-

cance of the archaeologically recovered material culture from the Middle Woodland component of the site is then compared to ethnographically derived models.

Finally, an interpretation is offered to account for the postulated social organization in terms of the economic patterns and the distribution of culturally similar materials throughout a vast and ecologically similar zone. To some extent the initial problems are still unanswered. Only further archaeological work on small single component or stratified sites in this area can test the derived hypotheses concerning the full seasonal cycle of resource utilization.

# 2. Environment

The Summer Island site lies on a series of meadow-covered sand dunes rising about twenty feet above the level of Summer Harbor on the northeast side of the island. Summer Island lies about three miles south of Point Detour and is northernmost in the island chain between Michigan's Garden Peninsula and Wisconsin's Door Peninsula, separating Green Bay and Bay de Noc from Lake Michigan (Figure 1).

Topographically, the island consists of a two-tiered outcrop of the Silurian dolomites which forms the western edge of the Niagara Escarpment (Plate I). Pro-glacial lakes have cut a number of terraces above the current lake level in the bedrock and the thin pleistocene sedimentary mantle (Brose, n.d.a). Above and within these deposits some thin soils have formed sporadically in the interior level areas of the island. But the bedrock outcrops are ubiquitous and, with the exception of the Summer Harbor area itself, meadow soils are rare (Brose, n.d.b).

Offshore, the lake bottom consists of broken and jumbled bedrock and large blocks of weathered dolomite. The bottoms shoal outward from the island at shallow depths for several hundred feet. The coastline of the island presents a formidable appearance, with blocks of colomite dropping a sheer 10-12 feet onto the more level rock shelves which form the shoals. There are two exceptions to this picture. At the extreme northwestern point of Summer Island is a low, gravelly bar extending to the north and gently dipping to about four feet below the water midway between the Summer Island. Toward the foot of Summer Harbor, where the bottom is less

than eight feet in depth, it is composed of a rather clean sand which extends shoreward to the beach. Nonetheless, scattered blocks of dolomite often lie inches below the surface of the water and along the sand beach. The beach itself runs along the southwestern shore of Summer Harbor (Figure 2) for 900-1,000 feet. To either side the limestone rises directly from the water to heights of from four to seven feet. Behind the sand beach and the 26-foot wide sand and gravel shingle, the land slopes steeply upward in a high sand bank, reaching a rather sudden plateau about twenty feet above the lake, This sandy plain forms a clearing, erratically covered with thin vegetation. The clearing runs along the harbor for about 650 feet north and south and is about 250 feet wide at the center. It is crescentic, following the shoreline, each tapered end meeting a limestone ledge and, immediately beyond, the forest. It is within this clearing that the Summer Island Site (Figure 3) is located.

Summer Island lies in the part of the upper Great Lakes best characterized ecologically as a transition zone (Cleland, 1966: 5). Dice has shown that the "Canadian Biotic Province" is a zone where Carolinian and Hudsonian fauna overlap (1938: 512) and Cleland notes that Summer Island lies just within the southern limits of a "pure" Canadian Biotic Province (1966: Fig. 1, p.6). Both would describe the flora of Summer Island as mixed hardwood-conifer forest (Dice, 1938: 503-5; Cleland, 1966: 9-10). Cushing, however, makes the point that within this vegetation community composition varies with time and space to produce a series of communities

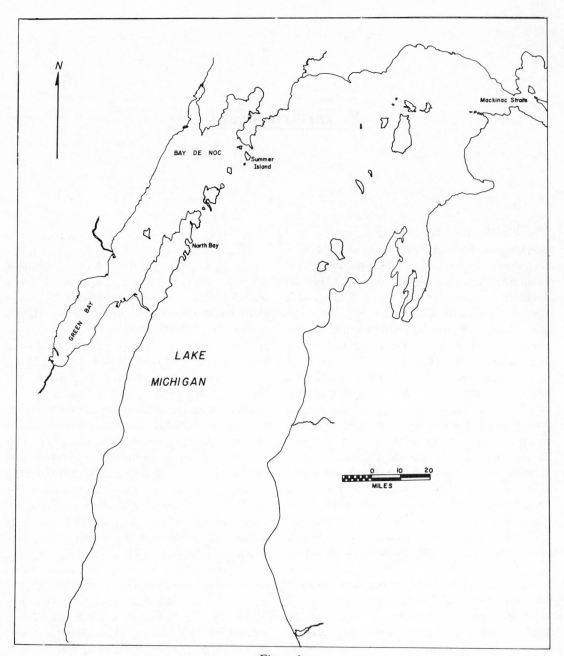

Figure 1

grading into one another, no one of which is by itself characteristic (1965: 407).

Forest cover in the island's level interior areas was characterized by a dominance of hemlock (*Tsuga canadensis*), balsam fir (*Abies balsamea*), beech (*Fagus grandifola*), sugar maple (*Acer saccharum*), paper and yellow birch (*Betula papyrifera, B. allegheniensis*). Other trees in this area were red maple (*A. rubrum*), white oak (*Quercus alba*), white pine (*Pinus strobus*), and basswood (*Tilia americana*). There was little undergrowth in this forest, and only two species, hazelnut (*Corylus americana*) and goldenrod (*Solidago*), were identified in any numbers. The more elevated interior areas were dominated by sugar maple, yellow birch, beech, and hemlock, with some basswood, quaking aspen (*Populus tremuloides*), red maple, rock maple (*A. spicatum*), white pine, and a few examples of black cherry (*Prunus serotina*). Undergrowth in these

Plate I — Summer Island from the North (Point Detour)

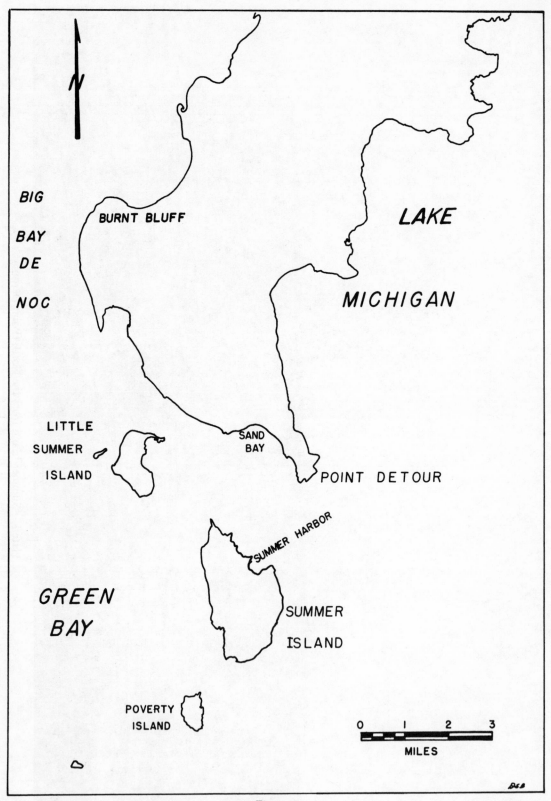

Figure 2

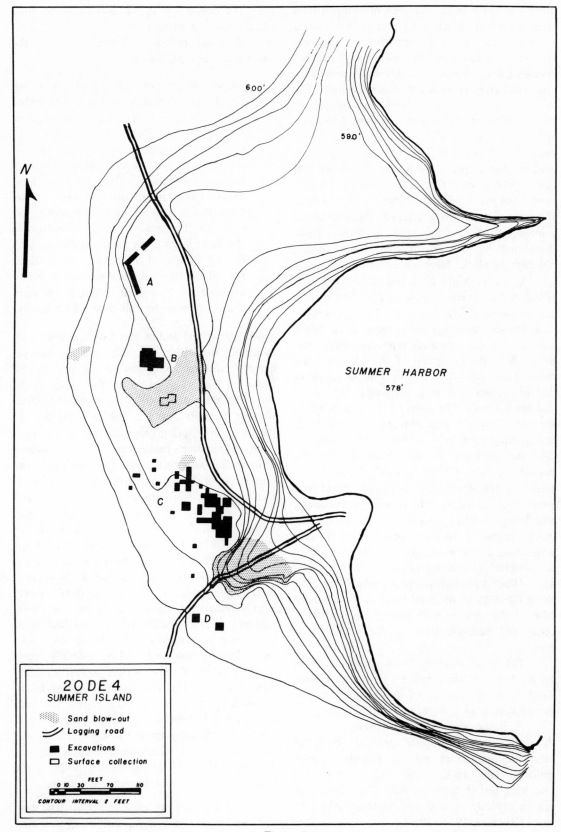

Figure 3

areas was quite thick and the following species were identified: black huckleberry (*Gaylussacia baccata*), red currant (*Ribes triste*), gooseberry (*Ribes oxyancanthoides*), blackberry (*Rubus occidentialis*), chokecherry (*Prunus virginiana*), and blueberry (*Vaccinium angustifolium*). Occasional flat clearings in these areas would be covered with goldenrod and milkweed (*Asclepias syriaca*). The slopes in these areas, where not bare rock, had a cover of jack pine (*P. banksiana*), quaking aspen, paper birch, and occasional red oak (*Querus rubra*) and fire cherry (*Prunus pensylvanicus*). On the rock itself, where little in the way of soils had developed, the weathered, jointed limestone supported a forest cover dominated by balsalm fir and white spruce, although hemlock, black spruce (*Picea mariana*), quaking aspen, white pine, red maple, red pine (*Pinus resinosa*), and occasionally northern cedar (*Thuja occidentalis*) occurred. There was little undergrowth, although there were dense windfalls; the damper low areas supported some blueberry. With the exception of the site area, the entire coast was covered with a dense tangle of northern cedar and with occasional balsam fir and black spruce. The edges of the area in which the site is located were covered by paper birch and quaking aspen, with northern cedar along the lakeward portions of the clearing. Directly behind the "screen," the spruce-fir forest characteristic of the Rock Lands occurred, mixed with paper birch and aspen. The clearing itself showed alternating areas of sand blow out, grass, blueberry, raspberry (*Rubus strigosus*), milkweed, goldenrod, sweet fern, (*Comptonia peregrina*), scouring rush (*Equisetum arvense*), and blackeyed susan (*Rudbeckia hirta*). Some chokecherry grew along the edge of the sand bluff at the southern edge of the clearing with several large northern cedar and hemlock trees in the north-central portion.

The total presently known mammal fauna on Big Summer Island consists of several insectivores, a small number of fur-bearing rodents, eastern cottontail, coyote, and whitetail deer.

A richer avian fauna is present, but of these the only seasonally available birds of economic importance are the Canadian goose, mallard, black duck, wood duck, pintail, and blue wing teal (Peterson, 1963). The island does not lie directly in any well traveled migration route (Hawkins, 1964: 206-7).

The only major faunal resource on Summer Island is the fish offshore.

Rostlund (1952: 73) has described the Great Lakes as a province,

> formed by the overlapping of the Mississippian and Canadian faunas, and therefore northern and southern fish intermingle in the region. Whitefishes, lake herrings, lake trout and pikeperch constitute the bulk of the resource which consequently is high in quality, for these fish are all prime food fishes. Other important fish are . . . pike, muskellunge, sauger, and lake sturgeon.
>
> In the smaller waters tributary to the main lakes or in narrow passages, such as the Straits of Mackinac, or at Sault Ste. Marie, the fish are seasonally highly available . . . aboriginal fishing in the main lakes may even be called an inland fishery.

Scott (1954) and Hubbs and Lagler (1961) have indicated that lake sturgeon, yellow walleye, sauger, freshwater drum, and burbot may also be found on shallow gravel bottoms or rocky shoals.

The shallow gravel to the north and northwest of Summer Island is the preferred bottom for such early spring spawning fish as lake sturgeon (*Acipenser fulvescens*), yellow walleye (*Stizostedion vitreum*), sauger (*S. canadense*), and burbot (*Lota [lota] lacustris*) (Scott, 1954: 7, 84, 86, 119). Northern pike (*Esox lucius*) and muskellunge (*E. masquinongy*) spawn in midspring in shallow bays, such as summer Harbor (*idem*: 75-77). The lake whitefish (*Coregonus clupeaformis*) and cisco and menominee (*Leucicthys artedi*) (*L. sp.*) spawn in November, preferably on rocky or gravelly shoals where large numbers of these species are commonly captured (*idem*: 19-22). The various lake trout (*Salvelinus ramaycush*) also spawn on rocky shoals in early November and are generally found in these same shallow waters with the spring thaw (*idem*: 34-35). To reiterate: Summer Island is unusually poor in terrestrial fauna the year around, but has unusually rich lacustrine faunal resources from early spring to November.

The climate of southern Delta County is described in a brochure published in 1925 by the Escanaba Chamber of Commerce as follows:

> The summers are most delightful. The days are comfortably warm, but, being tempered

by the cooling breezes from the three bays, the temperature rarely ever rises above 90 degrees ... The average annual precipitation for the past 50 years is 30.49 inches, falling principally during the growing season. Winter comes about the first of December and is followed by three to four months of crisp, invigorating weather. The snowfall averages from eight to fifteen inches.

While this picture is, predictably, optimistic (see Table I), it is reasonably accurate.

TABLE I  CLIMATE OF SOUTHERN
GARDEN PENINSULA AND
SUMMER ISLAND

| | |
|---|---|
| Average annual temperature | 40-45°F. |
| Average January temperature | 15-20°F. |
| Average July temperature | 65°F. |
| Average annual minimum temperature | -20°F. |
| Average annual maximum temperature | 95°F. |
| Lowest temperature observed | -40°F. |
| Highest temperature observed | 105°F. |
| Average annual precipitation | 25-30" |
| Period of maximum precipitation | April-Sept. |
| Average annual snowfall | 80" |
| Average annual number of days with snow cover | 120-140 |
| Average annual number of days with cloud cover | 140-160 |
| Average annual number of frost free days | 120-140 |

Source:  U.S. Weather Station, Garden Michigan
1889-1938 (U.S.D.A. Yearbook,
1941: 703-46).

A recent study indicates that the four months from mid-November to mid-March produced 49% of all storms during the period A.D. 1889-1961 (see Brose (n.d.b). In winter, northern Lake Michigan is covered by ice building out from shore so that 60 to 90% of the water surface may be covered.

Freezing may be a smooth process, or it may be a result of the piling-up of ice in ridges and windrows that may rise from 10 to 20 feet above water level, making any transit hazardous. Lake shipping is usually suspended by the first of December and opens again between the middle of March (in the South) and early April or even early May (in Lake Superior). (Powers, 1962: 37)

While the ice separating Summer Island from the Garden Peninsula is often thick enough to support a bulldozer it is subject to winds and currents, so that sections only a few yards apart may be less than one inch thick. Needless to say, this does little to decrease the hazards of winter travel. Considering all factors, the period from mid-November to mid-March is quite inhospitable on the offshore islands of Delta County.

# 3. Archaeological Excavations

The nature of the clearing within which the Summer Island site is situated limited the choices for locating the initial excavation units. All elevations below 584 feet above sea level along the shore of Summer Harbor were covered with driftwood, dead shad (*Pomolobus pseudoharengus*), and other flotsam, clearly indicating a storm beach. Directly west of this shingle the sand ridges rose rather abruptly to an elevation of 590 feet above sea level. On this 10% grade test pits revealed no artifactual material, either aboriginal or historic.

In early June I had recovered some materials from deflated areas along the southern logging road 120-200 feet inland. Following this road to the southwest and testing along its sand banks clearly indicated a decrease in the frequency of aboriginal materials from east to west after a distance of 150 feet from the harbor. The logging road running to the north paralleled the shoreline for about 300 feet at a distance of about 80 feet inland. Several test pits indicated that no aboriginal material was located to the east of this road. Large amounts of aboriginal material were found on deflated surfaces immediately to the west of this road and in the northern bank of the southern roadcut at a distance of about 100 feet from the lake.

From these indications it appeared that the site lay to the west of the north logging road. A surface collection of several deflated areas along the 603-foot Nipissing beach (just inside the woods, 200-250 feet from the harbor beach) revealed only historic material. A series of historic foundations at the northern edge of the clearing (Figure 3, Area "A") were tested and revealed sterile sands overlying the bedrock less than one foot below the floors.

Thus, the main prehistoric occupation seemed to be located in the 180 × 400-foot area northwest of the logging roads, east of the 603-foot beach ridge and south of the historic foundations. Within this area were several deep sandblows where surface collections had been made. A small test pit dug into each of these blows revealed that deflation had removed all overburden above the sterile sands. Since no occupation could be encountered in these blowouts, excavations were confined to the vegetation-stabilized surfaces.

All excavation units were identified by reference to the coordinates of their southwest corner. The location and elevation of this designator stake was surveyed in from lake level with the transit and rod, and all depth measurements within that unit were taken from a line marked on the stake at ground level. Each excavation unit was dug as a vertical-sided 5 × 5, 5 × 10, or 10 × 10-foot unit. Within the larger units all material was segregated in separate 5 × 5-foot squares, so that all excavation units represent a 25 square-foot area.

All excavation units were dug to remove each different stratum as a discrete provenience unit. That this ideal was not always attained is due principally to the extremely homogeneous nature of the several strata immediately below the sod. Where any change of soil texture or color was perceived in excavating, the surface of the new stratum was not violated, and the floor

12

was cleaned horizontally to reveal its extent. All artifacts were left in place on this interface and a plan drawing ("square sheet") of the unit at that depth was made to 1/12 scale. Depth, below ground level at the southwest corner, was measured for all corners and for any other points higher or low than the rest of the floor. The locations of all *in situ* artifacts were measured, and they were recorded by separate item numbers on this plan. The floor was watered down with a three-gallon garden sprayer, and soil colors were compared to those in the Munsell color charts (Munsell, 1958). The hue and chroma/value was entered on this plan map to indicate differential coloration within the stratum. All post molds and features were measured, recorded, and generally pedestaled until the next level or lower. If it seemed worthwhile, the floor was then rewet and a series of 2¼ × 2¼-inch black-and-white and 35mm diapositive photographs were taken.

All excavated material other than the midden levels and feature contents, was sifted through quarter-inch hardware cloth. The only exception to this was the 12-foot geological test pit that was dug through the botton of a previously excavated 10 × 10 foot excavation unit. The dense middens were sifted through eight-inch hardware cloth. In both cases, *all* material remaining in the screens was recovered. The entire contents of all features (pits, hearths, large post molds) were subjected to flotation. All flotation material and seventeen 500cc unsifted soil samples were recovered for microscopic analysis.

Wherever a change in soil color or texture indicated that a new stratum had been reached, the material recovered from the surface of the previous stratum to the surface of the newly exposed one was bagged separately and the provenience unit was closed. All provenience units were designed to include material from a single layer of soil within a 5 × 5-foot square. All features or concentrations of bone, chippage, sherds, etc. were given individual provenience designations. Where the edge of the midden cut across a level within an excavation unit, materials from inside and outside the midden area were given separate provenience designations. Where excavation cut down 0.3 feet without encountering any soil change, an arbitrary level floor was cut, a square sheet drawn, and a new provenience unit begun. All excavation units were carried down at least 1.5 feet into sterile sands; the early units were down over three feet into the sterile sands underlying the site. After each excavation unit had been carried down into the sterile sands the walls were shaved smooth, 1/12-scale stratigraphic profile drawings were made, and photographs were taken on at least two contiguous walls.

Because of the instability of the drying sand, sections of the wall frequently would slump when depths greater than three feet were reached. It was this factor that also argued against any attempt to leave large excavated areas of the site open and clean for medium-altitude comprehensive photographs of the house floors. As we were opening new excavation units by following the house patterns encountered previously, disposition of back-dirt was also a constant problem. The solution decided upon was to place the sifter tripods over the nearest excavated unit and thus avoid the problem of moving our back-dirt piles to excavate the areas beneath them.

The geomorphological analyses of the site clearly indicated at least four distinct periods of human occupation. Of these, the first three are aboriginal, while the fourth can easily be related to the fishing village that is known to have existed through the late nineteenth century. The initial occupation of the site area, the Laurel component, although intensive was the most spatially restricted, being limited to the southern portion of the site with its focus in southeastern Area "C". The second occupation, the Oneota component, was scattered across Areas "B" and "C" with its greatest density in northern "C". The last aboriginal occupation of the site seems to have been centered in Area "B," although some evidence occurred in Area "C" and southern Area "A". The historic fishing village is clearly centered in Area "A", but it is also the most extensive of all the occupations with material in all areas of the site. The Middle Woodland occupation will be considered in detail in the chapters to follow. In the final chapters, an integration of the data from that period will be attempted and cultural-ecological interpretations offered.

# 4. The Middle Woodland Component: Material Culture

## OCCUPATIONAL EVIDENCE

Before the first human occupation the site must have looked topographically much as it does at present (Plate II). A fairly level sandy meadow dipped down from the edge of the forest to the rather steep sand bank which dropped about 12 feet to a wide sand beach running for 150 feet along the harbor. It was on a sporadically herb-stabilized dune surface along the southern margin of the meadow that the initial occupation of the site took place.

This occupation is best evidenced by the deposition of a dense midden (Plate IIIa) which occurred as three separate lenses within Area "C" (Figure 4). All of these midden lenses lay at elevations of from 595 to 596 feet above sea level and appeared to occupy slight depressions on the surface of the culturally sterile meadow-covered sands (Figures 5 and 6). Such areas often retain moisture slightly longer than the more elevated portions of well-drained sand dune deposits and are commonly colonized by beach grasses and rushes (Odum, 1959: 260-61). The three definite midden lenses were all roughly oval shaped and lay in an arc of about 95° running from southeast to northwest. The southeasternmost lens was the largest and averaged 25 feet east-west by 60 feet north-south. The central midden lens was not thoroughly excavated, but seemed to be about 20 feet north-south by about 15 feet east-west. The third midden lens associated with this component was defined by several test pits in northwestern Area "C" to be about 15 feet east-west by about 20 feet north-south. All three occupied the same stratigraphic pro-

venience and were remarkably similar in artifact content. All were sealed by thin brown aeolian sands and rested upon sterile sands. No overlapping of midden lenses occurred, and since sherds recovered from one lens could often be fitted to sherds recovered from one of the other lenses, their simultaneous occupation was postulated. All lenses were from 0.2 to 0.4 feet thick and ended rather abruptly on their margins. No stratigraphic break occurred within any of these lenses.

Within each of these midden lenses post molds originated. These stood out clearly from the underlying pale sands. After the midden was removed by troweling the floor was shaved level to reveal the patterns taken by these post molds (Figure 4). The post molds, caused by the *in situ* decay of wooden posts, are probably somewhat larger than the original size of the post because of organic staining of the surrounding sands. I will refer in all subsequent measurements to the post mold itself although the need for some correction should be kept in mind.

The distribution of post mold diameters in the Middle Woodland occupation at the site displayed a clear bimodality (Table II). The two mean post mold diameters fall at 0.23 feet and 0.64 feet. The pattern made by the larger post molds was easiest to see in the southeastern lens, where two oval structures could be traced. Although large post molds occasionally occurred in subsidiary structures or inside the large structures (Figure 4), it is evident from Table III that there was a very difinite tendency to use these large posts as external wall construction elements. Using this information, a tentative

14

**A**

**B**

Plate II — Two Views of the Summer Island Site (A looking NNE; B looking WNW)

Plate III — Midden Floors and Post Molds from Middle Woodland Component

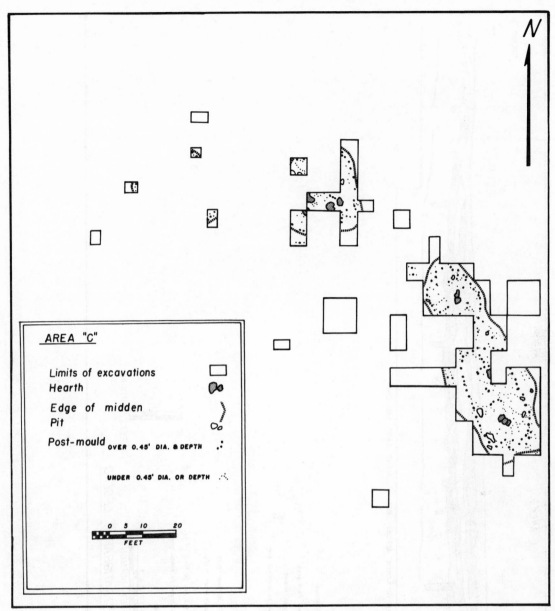

Figure 4

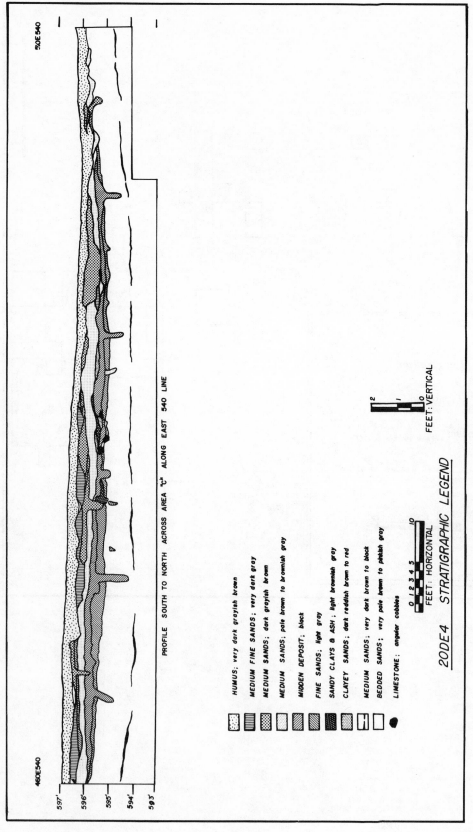

PROFILE SOUTH TO NORTH ACROSS AREA "C" ALONG EAST 540 LINE

HUMUS; very dark grayish brown

MEDIUM FINE SANDS; very dark gray

MEDIUM SANDS; dark grayish brown

MEDIUM SANDS; pale brown to brownish gray

MIDDEN DEPOSIT; black

FINE SANDS; light gray

SANDY CLAYS & ASH; light brownish gray

CLAYEY SANDS; dark reddish brown to red

MEDIUM SANDS; very dark brown to black

BEDDED SANDS; very pale brown to pinkish gray

LIMESTONE; angular cobbles

20DE4    STRATIGRAPHIC LEGEND

0 1 2 3 4 5                    10
FEET: HORIZONTAL

2
1
0
FEET: VERTICAL

Figure 5

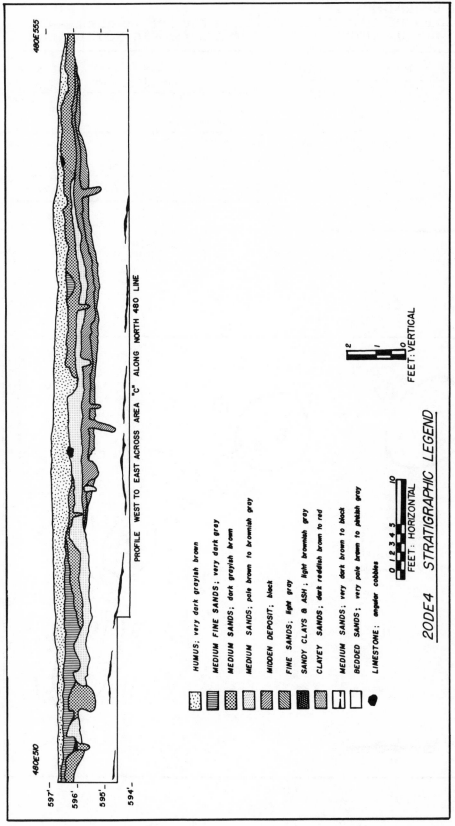

PROFILE WEST TO EAST ACROSS AREA "C" ALONG NORTH 480 LINE

HUMUS: very dark grayish brown

MEDIUM FINE SANDS: very dark gray

MEDIUM SANDS; dark grayish brown

MEDIUM SANDS; pale brown to brownish gray

MIDDEN DEPOSIT; black

FINE SANDS; light gray

SANDY CLAYS & ASH; light brownish gray

CLAYEY SANDS; dark reddish brown to red

MEDIUM SANDS; very dark brown to black

BEDDED SANDS; very pale brown to pinkish gray

LIMESTONE; angular cobbles

20DE4   STRATIGRAPHIC LEGEND

FEET: HORIZONTAL
0 1 2 3 4 5

FEET: VERTICAL
0 1 2

Figure 6

## TABLE II DISTRIBUTION OF POST MOLD DIAMETERS IN THE MIDDLE WOODLAND COMPONENT

| Class Limits (in feet) | Number of Occurrences |
|---|---|
| <0.16 | 9 |
| 0.16-0.25 | 47 |
| 0.26-0.35 | 89 |
| 0.36-0.45 | 23 |
| 0.46-0.55 | 24 |
| 0.56-0.65 | 49 |
| 0.66-0.75 | 33 |
| 0.76-0.85 | 10 |
| 0.86-0.95 | 3 |
| 0.96-1.05 | 2 |
| >1.26 | 1 |
| | 290 |

## TABLE III MIDDLE WOODLAND POST MOLD SIZE AGAINST LOCATION

| | External Wall O/E | Other O/E | Total |
|---|---|---|---|
| Over 0.45' in diameter and depth | 96/48.3 | 26/73.7 | 122 |
| Under 0.45' in diameter or depth | 19/66.5 | 149/101.5 | 168 |
| Total | 115 | 175 | 290 |

$$x^2 = 126.1$$
$$df = 1$$
$$p \lll .001$$
$$_2 = .4358$$

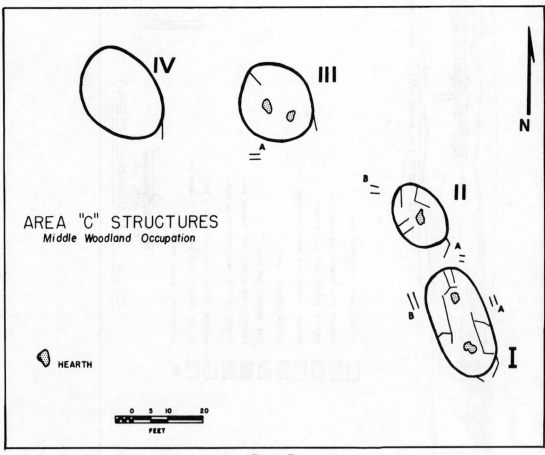

AREA "C" STRUCTURES
Middle Woodland Occupation

HEARTH

0  5  10      20
FEET

N

Figure 7

reconstruction of the structures in the central and northwestern midden lenses can be made. It seems reasonable to infer that four closed structures with a number of smaller open structures existed during this period of occupation (Figure 7). Only two post molds showed any signs of replacement of the original posts. Both involved the replacement of a small interior post by a larger one, and revealed a faint post mold about 0.35 feet in diameter cut by a larger dark post mold about 0.5 feet in diameter, resulting in a two-toned figure eight. The direct replacement of a smaller post for a larger one would have been totally unstable. It is possible that several other large-for-small post replacements took place with no subsequent archaeological traces. Such post replacement seems to be more in the nature of post-construction correction than repair, which would probably have utilized replacement materials of a size similar to the original. Accordingly, there is no evidence for replacement due to deterioration represented in these structures. Given the maximum of four or five years for the replacement of untreated fence posts on the Garden Peninsula, five miles away, it is assumed that this component at the site represents no more than two or three years occupation.

With little difficulty the four enclosed structures of Area "C" (see Figure 7) can be considered houses. The southern house in the southeastern midden lens (House I) was elliptical, with its northwest-southeast axis about 29 feet long and about 12 feet wide. At the foci of this ellipse two hearths were located. Associated with this house were two parallel rows of posts to the east and northwest representing open structures, designated ancillary Structures $I_A$ and $I_B$ respectively. Structure $I_A$ was four feet long and two feet wide. Structure $I_B$ was five feet long and two feet wide.

Eight feet to the north-northwest of House I, within the same midden lens, House II was oval in shape with a northwest-southeast axis 18 feet long and about 12 feet wide. A single hearth was located just south of the center. Associated with this house to the southeast and northwest were ancillary Structures $II_A$ and $II_B$ respectively. Structure $II_A$ was two feet long and two feet wide. Structure $II_B$ was four feet long and two feet wide.

Thirty-two feet to the northwest of House II, in the central midden lens, House III was located. This house seemed to be ellipsoid in shape with the northwest-southeast axis probably about 22 feet long and about 26 feet wide. Two hearths were located just south of the foci of this ellipsoid. Associated with this house was ancillary Structure $III_A$. Like the others, it was composed of double line of posts about four feet long and two feet apart. While imperfectly known, Structure IV was located in the northwestern midden lens about 20 feet west of Structure III. No associated subsidiary structures were recovered. No hearths were found in the excavated marginal portions of this structure, nor are any to be expected so near an external wall. If size can be taken as any indication, this structure should contain one hearth.

It should occasion no great surprise that the limits of the midden did not correspond precisely with the house walls. Numerous examples of Upper Paleolithic settlements are known where there is a sharp "edge" to cultural materials lying outside the actual walls of the structure. In some places the midden outside the dwelling is denser than comparable areas within the structures (Grigor'ev, 1967: 346). The most acceptable explanation for the distribution of these midden lenses at the Summer Island site is to be first sought in the distribution of the pre-occupation vegetation. The higher areas between midden lenses would have been subjected to stronger winds, as well as receiving less moisture, and therefore supported far less vegetation (see Odum, 1959: 256). Secondly, Schoolcraft reports that among the Ojibwa the usual lodge was an eliptical/oval framework of poles tied together at the top and covered with bark. About the border of the lodge on the ground twigs of spruce or hemlock were strewn, upon which skins were often spread for beds (cited in Morgan, 1881: 117). This seems to parallel the situation seen in the structures of Summer Island's Middle Woodland component. Add to this the tendency for sheet runoff to accumulate soluble organic compounds in depressions (*Soil Survey Manual*, 1962: 255), and the distribution of the midden lens edges beyond the borders of the houses is almost expectable. It may also be the case that these midden areas outside the houses represent the areas of the most intense human activity during this occupation. From this point of view they may serve to limit areas of constant traffic, crushing the extant vegetation and adding large amounts of exotic organic materials. This assumption will be returned to later when efforts are made to derive estimates of the population from the archaeological remains along lines suggested by Cook and Heizer (1965).

The four houses and their ancillary structures, found to have been simultaneously occupied over a two to three-year period, will be described in greater detail in the chapter concerned with the spatial distribution of cultural materials. First, however, it is necessary to present some analysis of the artifacts associated with this occupation.

## CERAMICS

From the 1967 excavations a total of 4451 sherds (wt. = 6347 grams) were recovered within the Middle Woodland levels of the site. An additional 163 rimsherds and 209 decorated bodysherds typologically assignable to this occupation were recovered from overlying levels. In the following discussions of horizontal distribution only those sherds recovered in position within their original levels of deposition will be considered. The distribution of ceramics from the Middle Woodland levels of the site are shown in Table IV by types and varieties.

As Table V demonstrates, the Middle Woodland ceramics from succeeding levels of the

## TABLE IV   CERAMICS FROM MIDDLE WOODLAND COMPONENT

| Ceramic Variety | Rim- Sherds | Decorated Bodysherds | No. of Minimal Vessels | Percent of Minimal Vessels | No. of All Assignable Sherds | Percent of Assignable Sherds | Mean Vessel Occurrence Per Excavation Unit |
|---|---|---|---|---|---|---|---|
| Banked Stamp, Plain, Oblique | 42 | 135 | 21 | 15.8 | 177 | 12.5 | 1.187 |
| Banked Stamp, Narrow | 22 | 51 | 14 | 10.5 | 73 | 5.3 | 0.679 |
| Plain, Unbossed, Notched | 89 | — | 13 | 9.8 | 89 | 6.3 | 0.418 |
| Banked Stamp, Dentate | 28 | 87 | 13 | 9.8 | 105 | 7.3 | 0.396 |
| Dragged Stamp, Dentate | 42 | 156 | 12 | 9.1 | 198 | 13.9 | 0.343 |
| Dragged Stamp, Plain | 87 | 342 | 11 | 8.4 | 429 | 30.4 | 0.291 |
| Banked Punctate, Fingernail | 7 | 26 | 11 | 8.4 | 33 | 2.3 | 0.261 |
| Braided Cord Linear Stamped | 15 | 37 | 8 | 5.9 | 52 | 3.9 | 0.269 |
| Banked Stamp, Plain, Chevron | 7 | 26 | 6 | 4.5 | 33 | 2.3 | 0.276 |
| Linear Stamped, Dentate Tool | 8 | 14 | 5 | 3.7 | 22 | 1.5 | 0.090 |
| Banked Stamp, Narrow, Beaded | 12 | 52 | 5 | 3.7 | 64 | 4.8 | 0.224 |
| Linear Incised, Interrupted | 13 | 17 | 4 | 2.9 | 30 | 2.2 | 0.030 |
| Miscellaneous Stamped | 12 | 30 | 4 | 2.9 | 42 | 2.9 | 0.007 |
| Linear Incised, Simple Criss-cross | 3 | 32 | 3 | 2.2 | 22 | 1.5 | 0.090 |
| Indeterminate | — | 21 | 3 | 2.2 | 21 | 1.4 | 0.060 |
| Totals | 379 | 1026 | 133 | 99.8 | 1462 | 99.5 | $\overline{X}$ = 0.309 |

TABLE V   MIDDLE WOODLAND CERAMICS BY
PERCENT OF VESSEL FROM COMPONENT

| Ceramic Variety, O/E | Middle Woodland | Mississippian | Late Woodland | Historic | Total |
|---|---|---|---|---|---|
| Banked Stamp, Plain | 16/15.7 | 18/15.7 | 14/15.7 | 15/15.7 | 63 |
| Banked Stamp, Narrow | 11/12 | 12/12 | 12/12 | 13/12 | 48 |
| Plain, Unbossed, Notched | 10/10.3 | 11/10.3 | 9/10.3 | 11/.03 | 41 |
| Banked Stamp, Dentate | 10/11.7 | 12/11.7 | 13/11.7 | 12/11.7 | 47 |
| Dragged Stamp, Dentate | 9/8.3 | 8/8.3 | 8/8.3 | 10/8.3 | 35 |
| Dragged Stamp, Plain | 9/7.2 | 6/7.2 | 8/7.2 | 7/7.2 | 29 |
| Banked Punctate, Fingernail | 8/7;5 | 7/7.5 | 6/7.2 | 9/7.5 | 30 |
| Braided Cord Linear Stamped | 6/6 | 5/6 | 8/6 | 5/6 | 24 |
| Banked Stamp, Plain, Chevron | 5/4 | 4/4 | 4/4 | 3/4 | 16 |
| Dentate Tool Linear Stamped | 4/3.7 | 5/3.7 | 3/3.7 | 3/3.7 | 15 |
| Other | 13/11.7 | 12/11.7 | 15/11.7 | 12/11.7 | 47 |
| Total | 100 | 100 | 100 | 100 | 400 |

$$\chi^2 = 12.207$$
$$df = 30$$
$$p > 90$$
$$\phi^2 = .0305$$

site do not differ significantly enough to raise any suggestion that they are not drawn from the same population.

In analyzing this sample, rim and body-sherds were merged to form a minimum number of vessels. Similar rimsherds and bodysherds were tested against these vessels and considered a separate vessel only if two or more attributes differed. This was considerably simplified by several characteristics exhibited by the ceramics from the Middle Woodland component at Summer Island: all vessels were plain-surfaced below the shoulder. Below the exterior lips all vessels exhibited only a single decorative technique exclusive of a single horizontal row of punctates just above the shoulder. Although angle and pressure of application varied, only a single implement seems to have been employed in the decoration of any one vessel. Finally we were fortunate in being able to reconstruct at least one vessel of almost each type from the lip to well below the shoulder. A detailed formal analysis of the proposed ceramic types and varieties has previously been published (Brose, n.d.b) with illustrations, and representative sherds are here illustrated in Plate IV.

All vessels displaying similar rim profiles, lip treatment, decorative motif, decorative technique, and design element, were considered to represent a single type. Varieties of this type were proposed where only implementation of decorative technique differed. Where orientation of design elements seemed to show clear differences, separate groups within the variety were set up (Table VI).

This method for segregating ceramic decoration may seem needlessly compartmentalized, but it was felt to be necessary in view of the fact that practically every vessel from this component has counterparts recovered from other sites which have been illustrated under a plethora of type and variety names. In most cases these *taxa* have been rather loosely applied, and the same material often falls into several different type-variety groups. Under the same name several different attribute combinations are unfortunately lumped together for purposes of discussion. James Wright (1967: 3) has claimed that, short of a detailed description of each sherd, such a method for attribute analysis is as good as any other. Spaulding, however, has demonstrated that certain combinations of attributes may be statistically more significant than others (1953: 305). In his application of Spaulding's methods to the Laurel ceramics of Minnesota, Stoltman (1962: 25-28) has agreed that the recognition of the attributes to be tested still involved a subjective element. It may also be noted that the discrimination of attributes may be as much a factor of application as of perception. In the reports alluded to above, a great variety of ceramic decoration was under analysis.

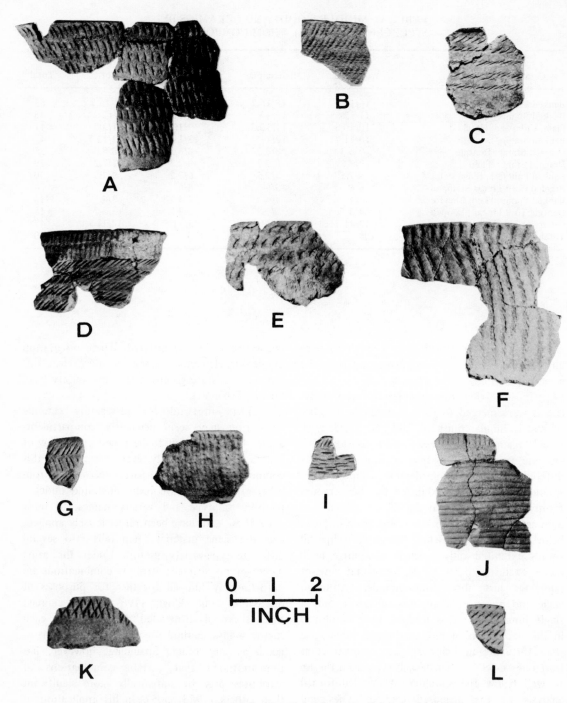

Plate IV — Varieties of Middle Woodland Ceramics from Summer Island

A. Banked Stamp Plain tool (oblique)
B. Banked Stamp Dentate tool
C. Banked Stamp Narrow tool (vertical)
D. Dragged Stamp Plain tool
E. Banked Punctate—Fingernail
F. Linear Impressed Braided cord

G. Banked Stamp Plain Tool (chevron)
H. Linear Impressed Dentate Tool
I. Banked Stamp Narrow tool Bedded
J. Linear Incised, Interrupted
K. Linear Incised Criss-Cross
L. Dragged Stamp Dentate tool

TABLE VI   SCHEMATIC REPRESENTATION OF
MIDDLE WOODLAND CERAMIC TAXONOMY

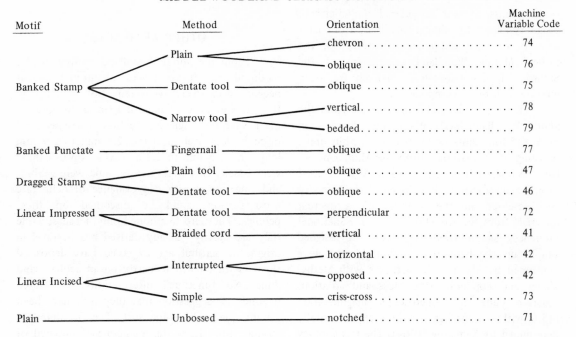

| Motif | Method | Orientation | Machine Variable Code |
|---|---|---|---|
| Banked Stamp | Plain | chevron | 74 |
| | | oblique | 76 |
| | Dentate tool | oblique | 75 |
| | Narrow tool | vertical | 78 |
| | | bedded | 79 |
| Banked Punctate | Fingernail | oblique | 77 |
| Dragged Stamp | Plain tool | oblique | 47 |
| | Dentate tool | oblique | 46 |
| Linear Impressed | Dentate tool | perpendicular | 72 |
| | Braided cord | vertical | 41 |
| Linear Incised | Interrupted | horizontal | 42 |
| | | opposed | 42 |
| | Simple | criss-cross | 73 |
| Plain | Unbossed | notched | 71 |

Minor variations within the "type" or "variety" were considered of little moment as the primary objective seems to have been to compare a number of types from one site to similar descriptions from other sites.

At the Summer Island site the ceramic population is of manageable size; the initial objective is to analyze differences in design elements and decorative motifs between areas within the site. Variation of style is quite limited. The range of variation is so limited in the Summer Island Middle Woodland component, that nearly 83% of all vessels from these ceramics would be classified as two types by Stoltman (1962: 45, 55), by Mason (1966; 1967), or by J. Wright (1967). Terms such as Becker Punctate, Push-Pull, and Dragged-Stamp do not convey the near identity of some of the sherds so described. Nor do they indicate the range of variation subsumed within each of these "types." For these reasons the discussion of the Middle Woodland ceramic complex from Summer Island will be in terms of the taxonomy outlined.

With the exception of temper particle size and sherd thickness, factors which are functionally related, these ceramics can clearly be considered as related to the Laurel Wares of Minnesota (Wilford, 1950; 1955: 133-34; Stoltman, 1962: 37-38), Manitoba (MacNeish, 1958: 138-54) and Ontario (Wright, J., 1967). In terms of the sherd thickness they seem to be more closely related to North Bay II Wares from the Door Peninsula of Wisconsin (Mason, 1966: 75-125; 1967: 280-302), the Saugeen Focus Ceramics from Ontario (Wright and Anderson, 1963: 23-36), and the Au Sauble Series from Michigan (Fitting, Brose, Wright, and Dinerstein, 1969). In view of the unresolved relationships of these ceramics, and to avoid prejudice by a too-ready assignment to established groups, a provisional series to be called *Upper Peninsula Ware* is proposed. This would include the Middle Woodland ceramics from Summer Island and similar ceramics from sites along the north shore of Lake Michigan as far east as the Mackinac Straits. The similarity of this designation to the Point Peninsula Wares of eastern Ontario and upper New York State (Ritchie and MacNeish, 1949: 97-106) is not wholly coincidental, and is reflected in the ceramic complex as well as in the terminology.

## CHIPPED STONE

From the 134  5 X 5-foot excavation units at the site yielding *in situ* Middle Woodland material, 33,718 pieces of chipped stone with a total weight of 64,205 grams were recovered. With the exception of eight corner-notched projectile points, it was considered prejudicial to assign typologically similar materials from later deposits to this component. Nonetheless, the earliest Middle Woodland component of the Summer Island site should be relatively free from mixture with other components.

The entire chipped stone sample from the Middle Woodland levels of the site was analyzed by 5 X 5-foot units or by features within units. A listing of all materials from the Middle Woodland occupation is given in Table VII. Detailed formal analyses of each chipped stone category are presented in the analysis of artifactual materials from the site (Brose, n.d.b). Functional inferences as to tool use were not assigned simply on the basis of morphology, but were confirmed by staining the artifacts with Methyl Violet and comparing the gloss and striations observed under low microscopic magnification (45X) with oblique light to those experimentally determined by Semenov (1964). The terminology and classification of these materials do not differ significantly from those in previously published reports (Binford and Quimby, 1963; White,

1963, 1968; Fitting, 1966, 1968b; McPherron, 1967; Brose, n.d.b).

## OTHER ARTIFACTS

From the Middle Woodland component, 56 modified or altered pieces of ground and/or pecked stone were recovered. Not included in this number were 17 small flat (mean thickness 5 mm) waterworn igneous pebbles. These were all more or less oval in shape, 2.5 mm to 3.9 mm long, and 1.5 mm to 2.2 mm wide. Five of these were basalt, two were granite, nine were gabbro, and one was diorite. No evidence of deliberate modification could be discerned on these pebbles. They are mentioned only because, while they are clearly glacially derived beach gravel in origin, no natural agency could have deposited them in their cultural matrix on an aeolian sand dune. No functional interpretation is offered beyond the suggestion that they may have been gaming pieces of some sort. The 56 items of ground stone from this component consisted of hammerstones, anvils, mortars, pestles, abraders, net-sinkers, and manos. The rough stone consisted of fragments of specular and silicaceous

TABLE VII   CHIPPED STONE FROM  134 MIDDLE WOODLAND
EXCAVATION UNITS (WEIGHTS IN GRAMS)

| Category | No. | % No. | Weight | % Wt. | $\bar{X}$ Wt. | $\bar{X}$ No Per Unit | $\bar{X}$ Wt. Per Unit | σ N Per Unit | σ Wt. Per Unit |
|---|---|---|---|---|---|---|---|---|---|
| Flakes: | | | | | | | | | |
| Decortication | 5179 | 15.4 | 17300 | 26.95 | 3.4 | 386 | 129.1 | 543 | 213.3 |
| Block | 9837 | 29.1 | 14419 | 22.25 | 1.5 | 735 | 107.6 | 619 | 173.2 |
| Flat | 17682 | 52.4 | 15556 | 24.12 | 0.9 | 1318 | 86.2 | 2504 | 166.7 |
| Utilized | 223 | 0.66 | 922 | 1.44 | 4.1 | 1.68 | 6.8 | 4.25 | 14.7 |
| Bladelets | 88 | 0.26 | 89.2 | 0.13 | 1.1 | .62 | .61 | 1.47 | 1.5 |
| Chert | | | | | | | | | |
| Nodules | 16 | 0.045 | 105.2 | 0.16 | 65.7 | .12 | 0.8 | 2.17 | 14.3 |
| Cores: | | | | | | | | | |
| Pebble | 129 | 0.38 | 6707 | 9.55 | 52.3 | .96 | 50.1 | .89 | 119.7 |
| Block | 190 | 0.56 | 4966 | 7.75 | 26.1 | 1.4 | 37.1 | 2.0 | 107.0 |
| Bipolar | 259 | 0.77 | 2597 | 4.05 | 10.0 | 1.9 | 19.4 | 2.7 | 46.3 |
| Bifaces: | | | | | | | | | |
| Scrapers | 12 | 0.036 | 210 | 0.33 | 17.5 | .09 | 1.57 | .56 | 4.6 |
| Blades | 15 | 0.044 | 348 | 0.54 | 16.5 | .11 | 2.59 | .80 | 13.8 |
| Blanks | 12 | 0.036 | 256 | 0.40 | 21.3 | .09 | 1.92 | 2.31 | 8.9 |
| Points | 22 | 0.06 | 522 | 0.81 | 23.7 | .45 | 3.89 | .25 | 7.5 |
| Unifaces: | | | | | | | | | |
| End Scraper | 33 | 0.09 | 327 | 0.51 | 9.9 | .25 | 2.44 | .63 | 6.9 |
| Side Scraper | 17 | 0.05 | 172 | 0.27 | 10.1 | .13 | 1.28 | .41 | .4 |
| Notched Scraper | 4 | 0.012 | 39 | 0.06 | 9.8 | .03 | 0.29 | .17 | 1.9 |
| Totals | 33718 | 100 | 64205 | 100 | 1.9 | 2506.83 | 451.70 | 4670.13 | 1136.5 |

hematite, ocherous limonite (J. Wright's "paint-stone nodules" [1967: 34]), and cut and ground sheets of muscovite.

Seventy pieces of native Lake Superior copper, weighing 179.7 grams, were recovered *in situ* from the Middle Woodland levels of the site. Of these, 29 were finished artifacts while the remainder (weighing 79.55 grams) were unaltered raw copper or copper scrap. Not included in these counts and weights were two fragments identified as angular pieces of burned green epidote showing traces of copper adhering to Kewenaw basalt. This is the matrix in which the Lake Superior copper is normally found. The finished artifacts consisted of 14 rolled copper beads, three fish gorges, two fish hooks, four awls, two knives, two square-ended chisels, a copper flaking drift, and a small effigy claw or talon.

Eighty-four whole or fragmentary artifacts of worked bone were recovered from the Middle Woodland levels of the site. Twenty of these were too broken to assign to any functional category. The remaining artifacts comprised 10 flat (lenticular cross-section) awls, 17 round awls, eight mat-sewing shuttles, six toggle-head harpoons, three socketed points, and two flint-chipping drifts. In addition, 27 cut or ground beaver incisor chisels were recovered and a single talon of a Bald Eagle (*Haliaetus leucocephalus*) with a suspension hole drilled through from one side.

Detailed metric, morphological, and functional analyses of these artifacts as well as drawings and photographs can be found in the publication treating the material culture of the site (Brose, n.d.b).

# 5. Economy

## FAUNAL REMAINS

From all excavation units and features stratigraphically assigned to the Middle Woodland component, 25,430 grams of identifiable bone and 763 grams of unidentifiable bone were recovered. The breakdown by zoological classes were 13,667 grams of mammal bone, 9,356 grams of fish bone, 651 grams of bird bone, and 1,756 grams of other bone, primarily turtle. The majority of the 763 grams of unidentified bone is probably fish bone. Specific identification of all faunal remains has not been completed at this time, but the fish and mammal bone have been identified by Mrs. Barbara Luxenberg (née Bird) of the Museum of Anthropology, The University of Michigan. Following Cleland (1966) it is possible to obtain a more realistic picture of the focus of this economic adaptation by listing the available meat as well as frequency of identified bone for the various species recovered from this component (Table VIII).

Although bone preservation was quite good, the faunal remains from the Middle Woodland component were extremely fragmentary. This was especially true of the bird and fish bone and has rendered these bones unidentifiable to a far greater degree than the mammal bone. The bias that this may introduce to the analysis of the fauna will be increased by the greater amount of usable meat yielded by each individual which can be assigned to the identifiable mammalian fauna. This may result in a disproportionate decrease for the amount of non-mammal meat represented at the site.

The mammals recovered from the Middle Woodland component are essentially those which are found in or near Delta County today. The only exception is the moose, which has been retreating north with the clearing of the forests (Burt and Grossenheider, 1956). The presence of the moose and porcupine probably indicate that at the time of occupation the forests around the site may have had a high percentage of conifer (Cleland, 1966: 145). The presence of deer and the absence of many Hudsonian mammals clearly indicates that these forests were of mixed composition, paralleling the modern situation (Dice, *loc. cit.*).

In general, the seasonal inferences that can be made on the basis of the mammalian fauna indicate a spring or summer occupation. Cleland (1966: 163) has noted that the black bear hibernates from January until early spring and that though it was probably hunted the year round it could seldom be found during hibernation. The apparently heavy reliance on this mammal would thus argue for a site occupation between April and December. The presence of one portion of deer skull with the antler attached is evidence for occupation at some time during the late summer to spring period of the year, although a second fragment of deer skull has shed its antlers indicating a summer occupation. The large amount of identified beaver bone may also argue for a spring occupation (*ibid.*).

The fish fauna of this component is distinctly lacustrine, and the majority prefer clean rocky bottoms with cool water and little rooted vegetation (Scott, 1954; Cleland, 1966). The

28

TABLE VIII  IDENTIFIABLE FAUNAL REMAINS FROM
MIDDLE WOODLAND COMPONENT

| Species | Number of Bones | Minimum Number of Individuals | Pounds of Usable Meat/Individual | Pounds of Usable Meat/Species | Percent of Total Usable Meat |
|---|---|---|---|---|---|
| Bear | 8 | 1 | 210 | 210 | 3.31 |
| Beaver | 6 | 2 | 38.5 | 77 | 1.21 |
| Deer | 4 | 2 | 100 | 200 | 3.15 |
| Moose | 3 | 1 | 400 | 400 | 6.30 |
| Muskrat | 2 | 1 | 10 | 10 | 0.15 |
| Otter | 2 | 1 | 5 | 5 | 0.08 |
| Rabbit | 2 | 1 | 5 | 5 | 0.08 |
| Porcupine | 1 | 1 | 10 | 10 | 0.16 |
| ALL MAMMALS | 29 | 10 | | 917 | 14.28 |
| Sturgeon | 678 | 147 | 36 | 5292 | 83.57 |
| Walleye | 18 | 3 | 10.5 | 31.5 | 0.49 |
| Bass | 5 | 2 | 5.8 | 11.6 | 0.18 |
| Northern Pike | 2 | 1 | 14.4 | 14.4 | 0.22 |
| Sucker | 2 | 1 | 5 | 10 | 0.16 |
| Gar | 1 | 1 | 3.5 | 3.5 | 0.0005 |
| Drum | 1 | 1 | 2 | 2 | 0.0003 |
| ALL FISH | 707 | 156 | | 5365 | 84.62 |
| Duck | 8 | 2 | 3.5 | 7 | 0.11 |
| Loon | 1 | 1 | 4.9 | 4.9 | 0.07 |
| Goose | 1 | 1 | 10.5 | 10.5 | 0.16 |
| ALL BIRDS | 10 | 4 | | 22.4 | 0.35 |
| Turtle | 17 | 8 | 1.2 | 9.6 | 0.15 |
| TOTAL | 762 | 178 | | 6314 | 99.40 |

sturgeon, walleye, and pike in particular are spring-spawning fish and can be netted or speared in the clear shoal waters where they run from April through June (Scott, 1954: 7, 75, 84). The total absence of any identified whitefish or lake trout (which spawn from October to December (Scott, 1954: 19, 34) is negative evidence pointing to the spring-summer occupation of the site.

The avian fauna cannot greatly aid in fixing the season of occupation until the species of duck and goose are identified. It may be noted, however, that the loon can be found in the area the year around while, with the exception of blue-wing teal, the ducks and geese are only transients in the late fall and spring. If Cleland's observation that "... at this latitude turtles are good indicators of summer occupation ..." (idem: p. 148) can be applied to Summer Island as well as to the Mero site, the faunal remains would suggest an occupation from the first spring thaw to the first frost.

## FLORAL REMAINS

The floral remains from this component were identified by Daniel Caister and Volney Jones of the Museum of Anthropology Ethnobotanical Laboratory, The University of Michigan. These consisted of 12 fragments of hazelnut shell (Corylus sp.) and 23 chokecherry pits (Prunus virginiana). The hazelnuts are available August to September while the chokecherry ripens July to August (Yarnell, 1964: 59, 63). These would indicate that the occupation of the site extended throughout the summer. No cultigens were recovered from any deposits assignable to the Middle Woodland component.

Although considerable attention was given to the excavation of all features and to any area of the site which showed a denser texture than normal, no evidence was encountered for any sort of wild rice threshing pits such as those ethnographically reported for the Menominee or those in late archaeological sites (Johnson, 1969). The seeds of this plant are collected in September or later (Yarnell, 1964: 65). It may be that the inhabitants of the Middle Woodland component did not utilize this plant. A more reasonable assumption might be that the seasonal availability of wild rice probably marked the abandonment of the spring-summer fishing village.

## ECONOMIC ADAPTATION

It is perhaps premature to attempt to characterize the subsistence pattern of the Middle Woodland component at Summer Island in terms of Cleland's (1966: 42-45) focal-diffuse continuum. The very definite predominance of sturgeon in the utilization of faunal resources clearly indicates that sturgeon fishing was the primary subsistence activity at this component. Focal economies are characterized as those whose societies have directed their economic practices to the exploitation of one or a few similar kinds of an abundant resource (*ibid.*). This occupation must be considered primarily as one of a spring-summer fishing site. Perhaps the larger mammals were hunted later in the summer when they had recovered from the winter and when the sturgeon had ended their spawning runs.

With this stipulation it is interesting to compare the rather focal nature of the economic pattern seen at Summer Island with the contemporary North Bay occupation of the Mero site (*idem*: 145-56). Quite clearly, the Mero intermediate and lower middens (associated with the North Bay occupation) display a more diffuse economic pattern, with deer being the most important resource but with beaver and sturgeon also contributing. Cleland (*ibid.*) has described Mero as a summer occupation which for some reason did not make full use of the great amounts of fish which could be harvested during spring-spawning runs. If Mero and Summer Island are viewed as two types of functionally complementary sites, it is easy to see the Summer Island site representing the major spring-summer occupation for harvesting sturgeon and Mero and short mid-summer occupation by a small group who may have spent the earlier portion of the year at a site such as Summer Island.

There may also be early autumn sites for these people, located at shallow inland lakes, where the major subsistence resource would be wild rice, or located on shallow sandy or gravelly bays of the Great Lakes, where fall-spawning whitefish, cisco, and lake trout could be taken (see Scott, 1954: 19, 21-22, 34). The latter type of site may be represented by the Heron Bay and the Naomikong Point sites on Lake Superior (Janzen, 1968; J. Wright, 1967: 41). The wild rice gathering sites would probably be similar to these reported for many of the Point Peninsula components in Ontario and upper New York State (Ritchie, 1949; 1965). Winter sites would probably be quite small and located along rivers or interior lakes. The major subsistence resources at these sites would most likely be mammals, probably the moose and beaver characteristic of the Canadian Biotic Province (Dice, *loc. cit.*; Cleland, *loc. cit.*). Numerous sites of this type have been reported from southern Ontario (J. Wright, 1967: 94).

The total economic pattern of the Summer Island population would seem to probably have placed its reliance on numerous and varied subsistence resources at various times of seasonal availability. While any single site will produce archaeological evidence for what in Cleland's terms would be a focal economic pattern, the total adaptation of the culture would clearly be diffuse. Cleland noted this fact and went on to state that this type of diffuse economic adaptation required the culture practicing it to have a large technological inventory and to be extremely mobile (*idem*: 44). This would go far to explain the wide distribution of sites showing similar archaeological styles in ceramics but quite definite differences in chipped stone and copper tools. Some of these can probably be interpreted as functional differences related to the different resources being exploited at different seasonal occupations. The mobility posited by Cleland is reflected in the thousand-mile range for similar archaeological materials in the Laurel to Point Peninsula continuum which occupies this ecologically homogeneous area of the Lake Forest Formation.

# 6. Middle Woodland Features and Structures

## FEATURES

The following features of the Middle Woodland component of the Summer Island site were pedestaled and excavated as discrete provenience units. Plan and profile drawings and photographs were obtained for each feature. Feature numbers were assigned serially as each was encountered, regardless of horizontal or vertical location. These numbers serve merely to identify the feature and have no other significance.

To conserve space and avoid needless repetition, all features will be discussed in tabular format (Table IX) as outlined below:

Feature
Number: Identifying features number, serially assigned.

Definition: Functional interpretation based on morphology, contents, and location of the feature.

Excavation
Unit: Coordinates of southwest corner of 5 X 5-foot unit or units in which the feature occurs.

Location: Association with other features and structures at the level.

Size: Maximum length X maximum width X maximum depth, measured from the highest level at which the feature was noted.

Shape: Relative shape in horizontal plane and vertical profile.

Contents: Material recovered from within feature boundaries, generally listed in the following sequence: (1) chipped stone tools; (2) retouched flakes; (3) bipolar cores; (4) weight of nonutilized chippage; (5) ground stone material; (6) bone tools; (7) mammal bone; (8) fish bone; (9) bird bone; (10) other bone; (11) copper material; (12) ceramics listed by number of sherds from named groups; (13) weight of fire-cracked rock fragments; (14) figure or plate designation, if any.

Most of the data in Table IX is quite self-explanatory. However, several feature require somewhat greater explication than the format allows. Storage pits, for example, were generally poor in artifactual material. They had a dark soil layer at their bottoms indicative of some degree of organic decomposition. What material they did contain occurred in a single thin stratum superimposed over this darker lens. Above this these pits showed a rather large homogeneous stratum of sterile sand which practically filled the pit to the top. Refuse pits, on the other hand, were filled with a large number of strata alternating rather light colored sands with darker strata indicative of organic decomposition. Artifactual material occurred throughout these deposits. The refuse pits contained a considerable number of fragments of fire-cracked igneous rock and faunal remains indicating their use of some period of time as an area for rubbish disposal.

TABLE IX  MIDDLE WOODLAND FEATURES

| F.# | Definition | Ex. Unit | Location | Size | Shape | Contents |
|---|---|---|---|---|---|---|
| 6 | Storage Pit (empty) | 460E540 | 7 feet from entrance along W wall within | 2'x1.5' x0.7' | Oblong: steep sided, asymmetrical | 1 retouched flake; 17 grams chippage; 70 grams fish bone; 2 sherds Banked Punctate, plain tool, (chevron); 2 sherds Linear Impressed, Dentate Stamp; 1 sherd Banked Stamp, Narrow tool, (oblique) |
| 15 | Refuse Pit | 475E545 | 10 feet from entrance along E wall, within Structure I | 1.5'x1.6' x0.6' | Circular: steep sided symmetrical flat-bottomed | 1 utilized bladelet; 11 grams chippage; 3 sherds Banked Stamp, plain tool (oblique); 0.5 kg. fire-cracked rock, |
| 46 | Refuse Pit | 470E455-450 | 7 feet from entrance along E wall, Structure I | 3.1'x2.8' x0.8' | Circular: shallow, asymetrical, round-bottomed | 1 end scraper; 3 utilized flakes; 8 bipolar cores; 591 grams chippage; 20 grams mammal; 80 grams fish bone; 110 grams other bone; 1 sherd U.P. Plain; 1 sherd Linear Incised; simple (criss-cross); 3 sherds Dragged Stamp, Dentate tool |
| 5 | Refuse Pit | 460E535 | 9 feet from entrance along SW wall, outside Structure I | 2.9'x2.3' x2.2' | Oval: steep sided, symmetrical, round-bottomed | 2 utilized flakes; 37 grams chippage; 9 grams mammal; 20 grams fish bone; 1 sherd Banked Stamp, dentate tool; 1 sherd Banked Stamp, Plain tool (oblique); 4 sherds Dragged Stamp, plain tool |
| 12 | Hearth | 480-485 E540 | NW Focus of Structure I | 3.9'x2.5' x1.5' | Oval steep sided symmetrical, round-bottomed | 1 thumbnail scraper; 1 utilized flake; 35 grams chippage; 5 grams mammal bone; 6 sherds Linear Impressed, Braided Cord; 1 sherd Banked Stamp, narrow tool (oblique); 2 sherds Dragged Stamp, Plain tool (oblique); 1.5 kg. fire-cracked rock |
| 45 | Hearth | 465-470E 540-545 | SW Focus of Structure I | 4.9'x3.9' x0.2' | Oval: steep sided, symmetrical round-bottomed | 1 bifacial blank; 1 bipolar core; 121 grams chippage; 1 bone "mat" needle; 68 grams mammal; 135 grams fish bone; 1 copper awl; 13 sherds Dragged Stamp, Dentate tool, (oblique); 8 sherds Banked Stamp, narrow tool (vertical; 1 sherd Banked Stamp, Dentate tool; 24.1 kg. fire-cracked rock; 3 sherds Linear Impressed, Dentate Stamp |
| 4 | Internal Platform | 470E535 | Between F. #45 and W wall 12 feet from entrance, within Structure I | 3.7'x4.6' x0.2' | Keyhole-shaped locus of post molds about a burned area | 190 grams mammal bone; 50 grams fish bone; 5.2 kg. fire-cracked rock; 2 sherds Linear Impressed, Braided cord; 1 sherd Linear Impressed, Dentate stamp |

## TABLE IX (CONTINUED)

| F.# | Definition | Ex. Unit | Location | Size | Shape | Contents |
|---|---|---|---|---|---|---|
| 38 | Refuse Pit | 475-480 E550 | 2 feet SE of Ancillary Structure Ia | 1.9'x1.3' x1.2' | Oblong: steep sided, symmetrical rounded bottomed | 32 grams chippage; 20 grams fish bone; 2 sherds Linear Impressed Braided cord (vertical); 15 plain surface grit-tempered bodysherds; 2 sherds Linear Incised (criss-cross); 4 sherds Linear Incised, Interrupted var.; 5 sherds Dragged Stamp, Plain tool |
| 2 | Drying Rack | 480E 525-530 | Ancillary Structure Ib | 6.4'x2.4' x0.4' | 2 long parallel rows of post molds | 1 bifacial blank, 1 corner notched projectile point; 4 utilized flakes; 1 utilized bladelet; 91 grams chippage; 450 grams mammal; 9 grams fish bone; 1 rolled copper bead; 4 sherds Banked Stamp Dentate tool; 12 sherds Dragged Stamp Plain tool (oblique); 6 sherds Banked Punctate Fingernail (oblique); 1.8 kg. fire-cracked rock |
| 19 | Refuse Pit | 505E535 | Between F #20 and N wall opposite entrance within Structure II | 2.3'x1.8' x0.9' | Circular: steep sided asymmetrical round-bottomed | 1 bifacial blank; 2 bifacial blades; 1 side notched projectile point; 312 grams chippage; 5 grams mammal; 30 grams fish bone; 2 plain bodysherds; 8.5 kg. fire-cracked rock; Chokecherry and Hazlenut |
| 42 | | | SAME AS FEATURE #19 | | | |
| 22 | Refuse Pit | 500E520 | 16 feet from entrance dug under NW wall of Structure II from within | 1.1'x0.9' x0.7' | Circular: steep sided asymmetrical round-bottomed | 1 end scraper: 4 retouched flakes; 337 grams chippage; 1 bone awl; 180 grams fish bone; 17 plain surface grit-tempered bodysherds; 4 rimsherds U.P. Plain, unbossed (notched lip) |
| 20 | Hearth | 500E 525-530 | Center of Structure II | 4.0'x3.3' x2.0' | Oval: steep sided, symmetrical round-bottomed | 1 thumbnail scraper; 5 utilized blades; 37 grams chippage; 5 bipolar cores; 1 net sinker; 1 state abrader; 2 bone awls; 40 grams mammal; 49 grams fish; 199 grams other bone; 3 sherds U.P. Plain, (notched lip); 7 sherds Linear Impressed, Braided cord |
| 29 | Drying Rack | 490-500 E540 | Ancillary Structure IIa | 4.9'x2.3' x0.4' | 2 parallel rows of post molds | 5 grams chippage; 10 grams mammal; 245 grams fish bone; 6 utilized bladelets; 3 bipolar cores; 1 ground-stone hammer; 1 ground-stone mortar and pestle; 2 sherds Banked Stamp, Dentate tool; 2 sherds Linear Incised, Interrupted var. |

## TABLE IX (CONTINUED)

| F. # | Definition | Ex. Unit | Location | Size | Shape | Contents |
|---|---|---|---|---|---|---|
| 37 | Drying Rack | 510E505 | Ancillary Structure IIb | 4.7'x2.9' x0.4' | 2 parallel rows of post molds | 1 utilized bladelet; 54 grams chippage; 20 grams fish bone; 45 grams other bone; 4 sherds Banked Stamp, dentate tool; 2 misc. Punctate; 2 sherds Banked Stamp, Plain tool (chevron); 3 sherds Linear Incised (criss-cross); 2 sherds Linear Incised Interrupted; 3.5 kg. fire-cracked rock |
| 23 | Refuse Pit | 52E495 | 4 feet from entrance within in Structure III, along NE wall | 1.8'x1.5' x1.6' | Oblong: very steep sided, asymmetrical round-bottomed | 1 bifacial blade; 2 bipolar cores; 88 grams chippage; 1 very abraded lump or specular hematite; 1 ground-stone mortar; 7 grams fish bone; 7 sherds Banked Stamp, Plain tool (oblique); 0.5 kg. fire-cracked-rock. |
| 32 | Refuse Pit | 530E495 | 4 feet from entrance within Structure III, along NE wall | 2.7'x2.4' x0.6' | Oblong: shallow, symmetrical, round-bottomed | 18 grams chippage; 1 bone awl; 10 grams fish bone; 6 sherds Plain, unbossed (notched lip); 3 sherds Linear Impressed Dentate Stamp; 6 plain surface grit-tempered bodysherds; 5 kg. fire-cracked rock |
| 43 | Refuse Pit | 540E480 | Along opposite wall 30 feet from entrance within Structure III | 2.3'x2.2' x0.8' | Circular: steep sided symmetrical round-bottomed | 2 utilized bladelets; 3 bipolar cores; 142 grams mammal bone; 145 grams fish bone; 8 plain surfaced grit-tempered bodysherds; 0.5 kg. fire-cracked rock |
| 44 | Storage Pit | 540E480 | Along N wall 27 feet from entrance, within Structure III | 1.4'x1.1' x0.6' | Oval: steep sided, asymmetrical, flat-bottomed | 19 grams chippage; 10 grams fish bone; 11 plain surfaced grit-tempered bodysherds; 1 kg. fire-cracked rock |
| 31 | Hearth | 525-530 E490-495 | SE Focus of Structure III | 2.3'x1.7' x0.8' | Oval: steep sided, symmetrical, round-bottomed | 11 grams chippage; 1 state abrader; 1 abraded lump of specular hematite; 1 bone awl; 25 grams mammal bone; 1 rolled copper bead; 5 kg. fire-cracked rock; 2 sherds Banked Stamp, Plain tool, (oblique); 7 sherds Dragged Stamp, Plain tool; 6 sherds U.P. Plain, unbossed, notched lip |
| 40 | Hearth | 530E485 | NW Focus of Structure III | 3.9'x3.4' x0.9' | Oval: steep sided, symmetrical round-bottomed | 1 side scraper; 2 utilized bladelets; 278 grams chippage; 30 grams mammal bone; 115 grams fish bone; 4 sherds Dragged Stamp, Dentate tool; 1.9 kg. fire-cracked rock; 1 sherd |

TABLE IX (CONTINUED)

| F. # | Definition | Ex. Unit | Location | Size | Shape | Contents |
|------|-----------|----------|----------|------|-------|----------|
| 40 continued | | | | | | Banked Stamp, plain tool (Oblique); 3 sherds Banked Stamp, Dentate tool; 7 sherds Linear Incised, Interrupted var. |
| 27 | Area of packed and burred lime and clay | 520E495 | In entrance to Structure III | 2.4'x1.6' x 0.2' | Oblong: very shallow lenses out at edges | 71 grams chippage; ground-stone hammer; block ground-stone anvil; 6 grams mammal bone; 5 grams fish bone; 5 sherds Banked Stamp, Plain tool (oblique); 3 sherds Banked Stamp, Plain tool (chevron); 35 kg. fire-cracked rock; 2 sherds Banked Stamp, Dentate tool; 2 sherds Linear Incised (criss-cross); 5 sherds U.P. Plain, unbossed |
| 1 | Drying Rack | 520E480 | Ancillary Structure IIIa | 5.8'x?x 0.3' | Two (?) parallel lines of post molds | 3 retouched flakes; 5 utilized bladelets; 6 bipolar cores; 728 grams chippage; 1 "net sinker"; 110 grams mammal bone; 48 grams fish bone; 1 copper fish hook; 125 sherds Dragged Stamp, Plain tool; 11 sherds Banked Stamp, Plain tool (chevron); 8 sherds Banked Stamp, Plain tool (oblique); 2.8 kg. fire-cracked rock; 2 sherds Narrow Banked Stamp |
| 36 | Refuse-filled depression | 490E535 | 3 feet E of entrance to Structure II, between Structure I and II | 3.3'x2.3' x0.2' | Irregular: very shallow; asymmetrical metrical irregular bottom | 1 end scraper; 4 retouched flakes; 40 grams chippage; 2 bone "mat needles"; 1 "net sinker"; 15 grams mammal; 35 grams fish; 20 grams other bone; 17 sherds Banked Stamp, Dentate tool; 1.5 kg. fire-cracked rock |
| 35 | Hearth | 490-495 E540 | 8 feet SE of entrance to Structure II, between Structure I and II | 1.8'x1.7' x0.2' | Circular: very shallow; symmetrical, flat-bottom | 2 retouched flakes; 33 grams chippage; 1 bone drift; 5 grams mammal bone; 1 shell pottery marker; 2 ceramic coils; 3 sherds Banked Punctate, Fingernail; 3 sherds U.P. Plain, unbossed; 5 sherds Dragged Stamp, Dentate tool; 6 sherds Dragged Stamp, Plain tool; 29 plain bodysherds; 6 kg. fire-cracked rock |
| 21 | Area of packed and burred clay | 495E540 | Between entrance to Structure II and F. #49 and F. #35 | 3.3'x2.7' x0.3' | Irregular: very shallow lenses out to edges | 1 bifacial blank; 2 retouched flakes; 1 utilized bladelet; 14 bipolar cores; 370 grams chippage; 2 abraded ground-stone hammers; 1 block ground-stone anvil; 2 grooved abraders; 1 copper awl; 1 copper fish gorge; |

TABLE IX   (CONTINUED)

| F. # | Definition | Ex. Unit | Location | Size | Shape | Contents |
|------|-----------|----------|----------|------|-------|----------|
| 21 continued | | | | | | 3 rolled copper beads; 8 pieces copper scrap; 1 fragment amygdaloid epidote |
| 28 | Area of packed clay | 495E535 | In entrance to Structure II | 2.2'x1.5' x0.2' | Oblong: very shallow lenses out to edges | 13 grams chippage; 1 sherd Linear Incised, Interrupted (opposed); 3 sherds Banked Stamp, Plain tool (oblique); 1 sherd Dragged Stamp, Dentate tool; 1 sherd Linear Impressed, Braided cord |
| 39 | Storage Pit | 490-495 E535 | 3 feet S of entrance to Structure II, between structure I and II | 1.2'0.7' x1.0' | Oblong: steep sided asymmetrical irregular bottom | 2 bifacial blanks; 1 bifacial side scraper; 11 retouched flakes; 8 bipolar cores; 822 grams chippage; 1 ground-stone hammer; 2 block ground-stone anvils; 1 antler punch; 20 grams fish bone; 1 sherd Banked Stamp, Narrow tool (horizontal); 5.2 kg. fire-cracked rock; 1 sherd Dragged Stamp, Dentate tool |

As there was no significant association found between the shape and size of the pit and the function to which it was put, the assumption is that all of these pits were originally dug for storage purposes but most were subsequently used for the disposal of refuse.

Hearths were distinguished from these pits by their larger, more regular, surface area, their lesser depth, and the fire-hardened reddish sands which underlay their central basin. These hearths invariably had a layer of ash, large amounts of charcoal, and fire-cracked igneous rock associated with them. A radiocarbon date of A.D. 250 ± 100 (M-1985) was obtained from a sample of cedar and aspen charcoal recovered from the southern hearth in Structure I (Feature 45). A radiocarbon date of A.D. 70 ± 280 (M-2073) was obtained from a sample of cedar twigs from the northern hearth in Structure I (Feature 12). A radiocarbon date of A.D. 160 ± 130 (M-2074) was obtained from a sample of unidentified charcoal from the hearth in Structure II (Feature 20). All dates show a clear overlap in the period A.D. 150-290. This is clearly an acceptable period for the occupation of this component and is in agreement with similar materials from Wisconsin (Mason, 1966) and Ontario (J. Wright, 1967; Johnston, 1968).

The features described as areas of packed and/or burned clay all were very thin lenses lying in the entrances of coeval structures. There was no evidence in any of these structures for a prepared clay floor, nor did these clayey areas display sharp edges indicative of deliberate construction. With the exception of Feature 21, these areas might best be interpreted as the result of heavy foot traffic which introduced some amount of silt and clay to these areas.

Feature 21 can probably best be interpreted in conjunction with nearby Feature 35. The latter was the only hearth area of the component not centrally or focally located within a structure. It yielded virtually no faunal remains and very little chippage of any type. It did contain larger than expected amounts of pottery and several very large fragments of fire-cracked rock. Also recovered from this small hearth were two ceramic coils, several lumps of fired clay, and a small piece of notched clam shell (*Lampsilis siliquoidea*). This notched shell fragment is considered to be a pottery marker used to create the designs observed on the Middle Woodland ceramics from this component. By varying the angle of application, the degree of pressure, and the edge of this tool used, the author was able to produce impressions on plasticene which would have been classified as Banked Stamp, Plain tool, oblique and chevron varieties; Banked Stamp, Dentate tool; Dragged Stamp, Dentate tool; Dragged Stamp, Plain tool; Linear Stamped, Dentate tool; and Miscellaneous Punctate. Feature 35 seems to have been a hearth clearly connected with the manufacture of ceramics rather than the preparation of food. Granted this inference, the explanation of Feature 21 would be that it represents an area where the raw clay was located prior to being modeled into ceramic vessels. The lithic and copper material recovered from Feature 21 indicates that the area was also used for male-related activities but it is assumed that this was subsequent to the female-related activity.

## AUXILLARY STRUCTURES

The features representing four of the five ancillary structures (Features 1, 2, 29, and 37) are all quite similar, varying only in details of size. These structures were five to six feet in length by two and a half to three feet in width. They were constructed of two roughly parallel rows of from three to five posts each along the long side. These structures are virtually identical to the ethnographic descriptions of cache racks, drying racks, and smoking racks of the seventeenth-century Chippewa (Blair, 1911: 275-76), and from the Upper Mississippi Valley in the nineteenth century (Morgan, 1881: 137, fig. 20). Racks of this type are still in use among the Round Lake Ojibwa (Rogers, 1962: B65-66) and the Mistassini Indians of Quebec (Rogers, 1967: 29-30; Plate II, B). All such racks from the Middle Woodland component at Summer Island are referred to as drying racks (Table IX), since there was neither evidence for additional side posts for the attachment of a cover for storage (*ibid.*) nor any evidence, in the form of fired sand or charcoal, to demonstrate their function as a smoking rack. If the relative amounts of animal bone recovered from these features can be considered partially indicative of their function, Structures $I_A$, $II_A$ (Feature 29), and $III_A$ (Feature 1) seem to have been used as fish-drying racks, while Structures $I_B$ (Feature 2) and $II_B$ (Feature 37) seem to have been meat-drying racks. Ethnographically the Indians of the upper Great Lakes have been characterized as

having preserved both fish and meat, "usually on racks made with poles for this purpose in order to dry them in the sun" (Rostlund, 1952: 195-96).

The most enigmatic feature from this component, Feature 4, was located within Structure I about 12 feet from the entrance along the western wall. Material recovered from a burned area within the post-mold pattern did not significantly differ from the surrounding areas. The configuration of the burned area corresponds closely to the post-mold patterns, indicating that the association is not a random one. The posts may well have supported a small platform within the larger structures, but the purpose of this platform and the associated burning are not understood. If this feature represents a small sweat lodge (as was first thought), its occurrence within a larger house is unique.

## HOUSE SIZE

The major structures already referred to as houses· occurred in two geographical clusters. Structures I and II were within about eight feet of one another as were Structures III and IV. The residential group of Structures I and II lay about 30 feet from the group composed of Structures III and IV. Within both groups two structural types could be distinguished. Structure I had approximately 280 square feet of floor space with two focal hearths. Structure II had approximately 210 square feet of floor space and a central hearth. Structure III had approximately 270 square feet of floor space with two nearly focal hearths. Structure IV appeared to have had a central hearth.

Densmore (1929: 22-26), describing the wigwams in use among the Chippewa of Minnesota and Ontario from 1905-25, indicates the structure was composed of poles ". . . planted in the ground, brought together in arches, and covered with mats. The framework was left on a camp site, and the coverings carried from place to place" (23). These structures were round or oval and of any size desired. Densmore photographed the construction of a small (12 × 9 ½-foot) wigwam in 1913. The illustrations (Plates IIIa, IVb) of the framework clearly indicate their similarity to the structures which were recovered archaeologically at Summer

Island. No list of the inhabitants was given for this structure of 124 square feet, but it was occupied by a single nuclear family. Densmore further indicated that extended families often occupied the same structure with each woman having her appointed part of the structure (*idem*: 73). She noted that

> the family usually comprised two or three generations living in a long wigwam with one entrance and a fire at each end, and a smoke hole over each fire . . . cooking was chiefly done at the fire presided over by the mother of the family, who prepared and served the food . . . A rack or frame was put near the door of the lodge.

> . . . Informants differed as to whether the mother's place was to the left or right of the entrance, but the daughters were always next to her. Each branch of the family had a possessive right to a certain part of the dwelling (28-29).

The sketch showing the arrangement of a typical family in a small wigwam indicates that the elders were furthest from the entrance (*idem*, 29, Fig. 4).

Hilger (1951: 138-41) described similar structures in use during the summer of 1930 and 1931 among the Chippewa of Minnesota and Wisconsin. She gives details on a number of such structures for both size and occupants. Two separate lodges 11 feet by 12 feet housed three people each. Two families were noted as occupying a structure 12 feet by 16 feet, but the exact number of inhabitants was not stated. Somewhat closer to Summer Island in time and space, Alexander Henry reported a lodge of 240 square feet occupied by a patrilocal extended family of eight (Quimby, 1966a: 161-64).[1]

If the average nuclear family is considered to contain between five and six people, the ethnographic example indicates that within the bark-covered elliptical lodge of the Great Lakes area the average number of square feet of floor space per occupant ranges from 22 to 100. Since both of these are extreme values reported from Round Lake (Rogers, *loc cit.*) the average figure for that group was also included. The results indicate means of 28.0 and 35.4 square feet of floor space per occupant depending on whether the extreme examples or the stated average was used for the Round Lake Ojibwa. If this estimate is reasonably correct then the number of occupants for each of the two types of structures can be inferred to be six or seven people for Structures II and IV, and 10 or 11 people for Structures I and III. Based on this estimate the

---

1. The elliptical to oval lodge built of a framework of poles tied together at the top and covered with bark or skins has long been reported as the standard form of dwelling in the upper Great Lakes. Lodges such as this were reported for the Menomini in A.D. 1673 by Marquette (J.R. LIX: 136); for the Fox-Sac in A.D. 1660 by Perrot (Blair, 1911: 309); for the Kickapoo by DeLilliet in 1684 (Quaife, 1962); for the Ottawa and Chippewa by Cadillac in 1700 (Kinietz, 1940); and for the Chippewa in 1764 by Alexander Henry (Quimby, 1966). In 1767, Johnathan Carver visited a Chippewa village containing about forty such houses, each having approximately 280 square feet and occupied by about twelve people (cited in Morgan, 1881: 117-18). Morgan (1881: 117) stated that a lodge such as this, about 16 by 10 feet, could easily accommodate two married couples and their children. T.T. Waterman (1925: 461-62) states that dome-shaped lodges among the Algonkian Indians ". . . in many cases had room enough . . . (for) a number of families and would contain, in addition to benches and sleeping platforms, space for a supply of food." Waterman illustrates an oval wigwam covered with rush mats and birchbark used by the Minnesota Chippewa in the nineteenth century (*op. cit.*: Plate I, fig. 1). The lodge appears to be about 12 feet in maximum dimension. The family standing posed outside consists of one adult male, two adult females, and four children. Waterman also illustrates a nineteenth century elliptical lodge 19 feet wide and about 40 feet long which looks very similar to the reconstruction of the Summer Island structure I. He notes this house was "Large enough to accommodate up to fifty people, as found among the Menominee, west of the Great Lakes." (1925: Plate I, fig. 2). Rogers (1967: 14; Plate I, B) describes and illustrates similar dome-shaped lodges still in use among the Mistassini Cree. He states that a large lodge might house one to four families while a small one, having approximately 120 square feet of floor space, housed a single small family (*ibid.*). Rogers also describes and illustrates the more common dwelling (with an elliptical ground plan) referred to as *inImicUwahp*, (1967: 7-12; Plate I, A). This is a communal dwelling, one of which was about 18 by 16 feet, and housed two families. Rogers states that this type of structure often had two fireplaces (*idem*: 12). Among the Round Lake Ojibwa in A.D. 1958-59, Rogers found floor space in their cabins ranged from 110 to 500 square feet with 22 to 100 square feet per occupant and an average of about 50 square feet of floor space to each occupant (1962: B65).

total population of the site was from 30 to 40 individuals. It should be understood that these estimates are tentative. Given the paucity of detailed ethnographic accounts of demographic and residential patterns in the Great Lakes area these estimates cannot be refined unless further ethnological studies are made, or until further archaeological work provides a larger sample against which to test them.

At the Middle Woodland time level, comparative settlement data is rare. Ritchie has reported an oval post mold pattern outlining a house 18 by 20 feet (287 square feet) with two hearths and an entranceway to the south-east, from the Kipp Island phase at Kipp Island No. 4 (1965: 246-47). At the Donaldson site Wright recovered evidence of an elliptical house about 18 X 13 feet (186 square feet) with a single hearth as well as a second structure he interpreted as a large rectangular house (Wright and Anderson, 1963: 11-15).

## HOUSE CONSTRUCTION

A detailed description of all the structures from Summer Island is not possible as Structures III and IV were only partially excavated. None of the data recovered from these two structures indicates any significant deviation from the patterns of Structures I and II. The following description will be based on these more completely excavated structures but should be applicable to the others as well.

In ground plan, these structures are oval to elliptical with a length to width ratio of about 3 to 2 for the smaller structures and about 5 to 2 for the larger structures. There seems to have been more attention given to keeping the width of the structure limited to between 12 and 16 feet than to maintaining a constant length to width ratio. This may be due more to the con-struction of these houses than to cultural dictates as will be brought out subsequently. The houses all seem to have had some sort of covered or screened entry extended three to four feet to the SSE. A similar orientation was noted for the Kipp Island structure as well. Rogers noted a southeast orientation for doorways among the Round Lake Ojibwa, but from his informants ". . . no explicitly stated reason could be elicited for the arrangement." (1962: B65). Prevailing winds from the northwest may well be the

reason the pattern has endured, if not the cause thereof.

The external walls of the structures were composed of posts, the archaeological traces of which had a mean diameter of 0.63 feet (7 5/7"). If an estimated value of 50% is acceptable for the relationship between the post mold and the original post, the mean diameter of the external wall posts would have been 0.31 feet (3 13/16").

The bases of these posts were roughly sub-rounded which may have been a result of their initial cutting. They were placed into the ground at an angle of about 15 degrees from vertical, all having their tops angled in toward the midline of the structure. These posts were apparently pushed directly into the ground with no evidence of bracing of any sort. Most seem to have attained a depth of about 1.5 feet to 2.0 feet below the surface. At this point in the con-struction the ends of the posts on opposite sides of the structure would be tied together to form a rough framework of arches to which the end poles are likewise fastened (see Cadillac's *Relation on the Indians* [quoted in Kinietz, 1940: 242]). Smaller horizontal poles, roots, or vines were then fastened to this framework and the entire structure was covered with woven rush mats, bark, or skins (Kinietz, 1940: 243-44; Densmore, 1929, 22-26). The floors of these structures, except immediately around the hearths, are assumed to have been covered with a layer of spruce or cedar boughs. As these were trampled into the earthen floor fresh layers of boughs would be placed about them (see Morgan, 1881: 117; Rogers, 1967: 26-27).

It would be reasonable to suppose that the posts or poles selected for the main framework would have to be rather supple to tie together without kicking up the unbraced end merely stuck a foot and a half into rather unstabilized dune deposits. This may explain the preference for saplings with a trunk diameter of just under four inches, and this in turn may explain why the width of the structure was not observed to be correlated with the length of the structure. A wider structure would entail longer, therefore larger diameter poles which would be much less supple and would thus require either deep post-holes to be dug, or some form of bottom bracing to be employed. The relationship between trunk diameter and usable post length will necessarily vary with the species of tree used.

## INTER-HOUSE STRUCTURES

Within the houses several large posts and numerous smaller ones occurred. There was no pattern observed in the large interior posts which would indicate their function as internal supports for the framework of the house. The smaller interior posts formed patterns clearly indicating rectangular substructures within the houses but since their height is undetermined it cannot be known whether they represent sleeping platforms, racks, shelves, or actual partitions. Some inferences as to their possible function can be made by considering the distribution of artifacts associated with them. In the following discussion referernce is only to Structures I and II which were more completely excavated than Structures III and IV.

In making the functional interpretation of these internal structures the following assumptions are made: the presence of a pit or hearth within any area enclosed by rows of posts is an indication that the posts do not represent a low platform which would have rendered the pit inaccessible; rows of posts which sharply separate functionally different areas of the house floor (as seen in artifact concentrations) are more likely to represent compartments or to have been partitions or screens than shelves or racks; rows of posts within three or four feet of an external wall and roughly parallel to it probably represent the interior edge of a shelf rather than a narrow corridor partition; and single row of posts unassociated with any parallel row or wall which do not separate functional areas probably represent a rack of some sort. These assumptions are based primarily upon common sense. The ethnographic reports which give detail of this sort (e.g., Densmore, 1929; Rodgers, 1967: 27-30) are quite compatable in all respects.

During the excavations in Area "C", as each strata was stripped off, the excavation unit materials in place on the surface of the underlying stratum were measured in from the designator stake and drawn on the floor plan. When the midden level was reached it was not shovel-shaved but was carefully troweled through and the location and depth of all artifacts encountered were measured and noted on the floor plan following the removal of the midden. Subsequent laboratory analysis was able to combine this data with the post mold patterns observed in the succeeding levels. This composite floor plan for Structures I and II is presented in Figure 8.

Within Structure I, immediately to the right of the doorway, a long shelf can be inferred. This shelf extends one to two feet out from the eastern wall having its western edge defined by a row composed of two rather large posts and three smaller ones. The northern end of this shelf meets the wall just past a refuse pit (Feature 46). Just to the west of this shelf is a rack, represented by a row of four small posts about four feet long, running NNW-SSE. To the north of the shelf described above, a rectangular area is defined by the east wall of the house, a row of five small posts crossing the refuse pit (Feature 46) and running west from the shelf for about five feet, a row of six small posts running north, and a row of three small posts which runs east to the house wall. Within this area a second refuse pit (Feature 15) occurred. This structure is inferred to have been a shelf. To the north of this shelf a row of three rather large posts runs west from the east wall of the house. Excavation did not remove the 5 × 10-foot area which would have allowed the complete substructure to be seen. As this row seems to separate an area of ceramic concentration from a relatively sterile area, it is inferred to have represented a curved partition or compartment, the far end of which is defined to the west of the unexcavated block by a row of two small posts extending south to a large post about seven feet from the north end wall. To the west of this row lies a roughly parallel row composed of three larger posts extending from the wall about seven feet to the fourth post. From this latter post a row of two posts runs to the west. From this westernmost post (which at some time was replaced by a larger post) a row of four posts runs to the south for about eight feet (parallel to the west house wall at a distance of about five feet) to where it meets a row of three large posts which extend to the west wall. This substructure is inferred to be another curved partition or compartment similar to that along the east wall. About four feet to the south of this substructure was a series of posts which seemed to indicate a rectangular shelf along the west wall over Feature 4. A small narrow shelf was inferred to have existed along the south wall just to the left of the entrance. It is represented by two large and two small posts. About six feet north of the southern hearth a

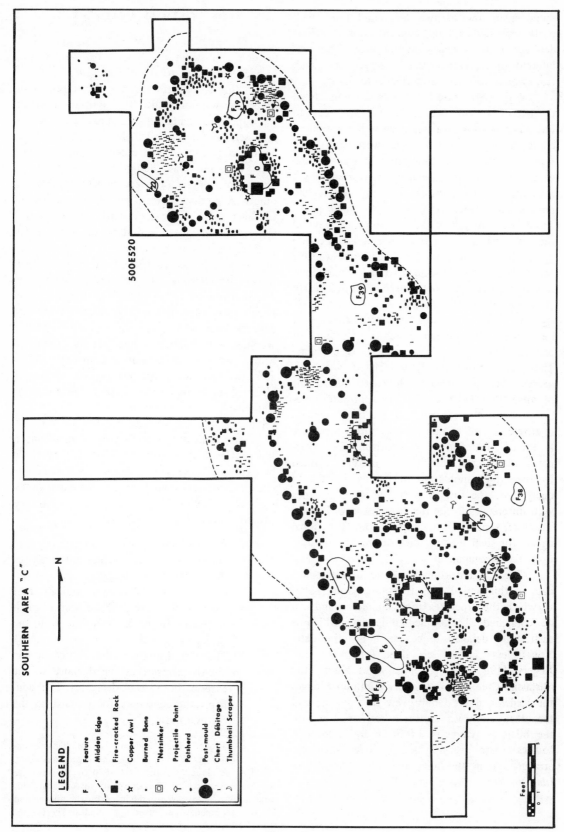

Figure 8

semicircular row of two large and four small posts separated a large concentration of chert debitage from a nearly sterile area. This was inferred to represent either a screen or a rack from which material was permanently hung.

Within Structure II the area immediately to the left of the entrance was unexcavated. Just to the north of this area was a curved partition or compartment parallel to the west wall. The southern edge of this substructure was defined by a row of five posts, and its interior edge by a row of five large posts (one of which had replaced a smaller post) and two small posts. Along the east wall of the structure, just beyond the only refuse pit within this house (Feature 19) an irregular shelf ran from the north wall for about six feet. There seemed to be a semicircular screen (windscreen?) between the central hearth (Feature 20) and the entrance.

In both structures numerous small post mold were encountered which no amount of playing "connect-the-dots" seemed to explain. These few posts closely associated with the hearths may have been employed to hold a spit of some type. For the other posts, no interpretation can be offered. While Structure II seemed relatively devoid of interior structures, Structure I seemed cluttered by comparison. The interpretations offered here for the patterns formed by these post molds are speculative indeed. In many cases the row of posts closely coincides with differences in the functional area within the structure, supporting the view of some functional nature for such substructures during the occupation of this component.

There is unfortunately little archaeological data of this period from the upper Great Lakes to which the structures from Summer Island can be compared. The ethnographic data which is sufficiently detailed to be useful is rather late. Nonetheless, Densmore's data (*op. cit.*) and Rogers' (1967: 21) statement that among the Mistassini Cree, "In two family communal lodges the leader and his family were on one side and the other family was on the other," may explain the bilateral symmetry of Structure I. In such lodges there were generally two fireplaces arranged along the long axis of the structure (*ibid.*).

## STATISTICAL ANALYSES

In order to study the way in which features and structures of all types were related to each other and to the distribution of artifacts within this component the use of electronic data processing was initiated.[2] The computer program was capable of handling an unlimited number of data sets of 80 linear variables each. No digital limit was placed on the coding of any variable. The program was designed to compute a regression analysis of every variable against all others. A product-moment correlation coefficient for each of the variable pairs was computed along with the mean and standard deviation for each variable. Finally, a test of the significance of the correlation coefficient (T-test) was performed to determine the probability that the co-variation observed was a result of sampling error. Each provenience unit was considered a separate data set with 134 sets for the entire Middle Woodland component. The results, discussed below, are not spectacular and merely add an aura of statistical confirmation to what was observed in the field or laboratory. The following statements should all be understood to have an r value over .422 and to have a T-test value of 2.6 or greater indicating that they were significant at the .02 level of probability. That is, they could be expected to show the observed co-variance by chance along less than twice in a hundred times.

The findings based on this preliminary structural analysis are as follows:

1) As the number and weight of fire-cracked rock in a refuse pit increases the number of different artifacts increases also. This may indicate that most artifacts are dropped near a hearth and tend to be thrown out with the garbage and rock.

2) The distance from the center of the hearth increases as the distance to the exterior house wall decreases. This confirms the central or focal hearth as the cultural norm.

2. Through The University of Michigan Computing Center access was obtained to a program called ISRMDC developed for the IBM 7090 by the Institute for Social Research of The University of Michigan. This program was subsequently modified by the author and Mr. Ray Lippman, an engineering student at The University of Michigan.

3) As the distance from the center of the hearth increases, the number of non-wall post molds increases. This relationship confirms the impression that the houses tend to have a relatively free central area, uncluttered by racks, shelves, or partitions. This indicates that the space around the hearth received the most traffic.

4) If two hearths exist in one house the southern hearth will be the larger in both diameter and depth.

5) The probability of encountering a refuse pit increases as the distance from the center of the house increases. That is, pits tend to be dug along the walls.

6) Within a structure the number and variety of artifacts within a refuse pit decreases as the distance from the nearest hearth increases.

7) Size and number of refuse pits increases as their location moves south within a structure. This statement along with statements 4 and 6 indicate that once emptied, the major function of the storage pit was to receive refuse from the hearth area.

8) The number and weight of fire-cracked rock not within pits or hearths increases as the distance from the center of the house increases. This may indicate that more care was taken to keep the area around the hearths relatively free from refuse. Most of this fire-cracked rock was against the inner edge of the house walls but no deliberate placement is inferred. Rather it seems as it those areas receiving the least foot traffic were most likely to accumulate refuse.

Finally, one might also note, although there was no statistical support, that the only two interior features which were not filled with charcoal, ash, and fire-cracked rock were apparently directly below shelves of some sort. In general, the ISRMDC program indicated the strongest associations were between features with faunal remains and with artifacts. These will be discussed in the following chapter.

# 7. Areal Distributions

## GENERAL APPROACH

Having decided upon the use of data processing machines for the analysis of artifacts in relation to features and structures within the Middle Woodland component, all artifacts, floral and faunal remains, and fire-cracked rock were assigned a machine coded variable number and entered on IBM cards. One hundred thirty-four data sets, each representing a discrete provenience unit, could be definitely assigned to the Middle Woodland component on the basis of stratigraphy. All materials recovered *in situ* as well as the material recovered in screening these units was included within the data set.

As the modified computer program was designed to generate linear regressions and product-moment correlation coefficients, non-linear variables could not be coded. Therefore, every artifact type for which information was desired had to be assigned a separate coded variable number which recorded the frequency of that variable within the data set (provenience unit). Since the program was limited to 80 variables, some artifact types had to be collapsed together to meet loading requirements. In the Middle Woodland data sets all floral remains were recorded simply as frequency of individual items recovered. Faunal remains had not at that time been identified as to number of individuals or species and had to be recorded simply by weight of recovered bone by zoological class. Since *in situ* measurements had been obtained on all finished copper artifacts from this component with the exception of three rolled beads, copper was recorded as two variables; either as the

number of finished artifacts or as the weight of scrap copper. Worked bone had not yet been functionally identified and so was recorded only by number of artifacts per data set. Lithic debitage was recorded by weight for flakes and cores since analysis had indicated mean weights of each of these categories tended to be quite constant at all areas of the site. Bipolar cores, utilized flakes, and bladelets were also assigned a second machine coded variable number as there was evidence that they functioned as artifacts rather than merely waste chippage (Brose, n.d.b). Fire-cracked rock, being extremely firable, was coded by weight rather than by number. All other lithic materials were given a separate machine coded variable number and were recorded by numerical frequency of occurrence within each data set.

## CERAMICS

*Initial Recordings.*—Ceramics were analyzed into types, varieties, and subvarietal groups, each of which was separately recorded by numerical frequency of vessels represented within the data set. That is, where two sherds representing a single vessel of, say, Banked Stamp, Plain tool variety (oblique group) occurred in the same provenience unit the digit recorded for that ceramic variable (76) would be 1. If two vessels of this group had each been represented by one (or twenty) sherds within that same unit the digit recorded would have been 2. In this manner the resultant correlations based on vessels would be between different ceramic modes (Rouse, 1939) and should thus be expressions of the areal distribution of culturally determined styles as visualized by the potters.

It is, of course, recognized that the correlations based on vessels as described above do not take into consideration the possibility that a single vessel may be represented in more than a single data set. To test the possible significance of this problem in distributional analyses a diagram of provenience units linked by matching sherds was made. A regression analysis plotting the distance between linked units (in class intervals of five feet) against number of occurrences of each class showed a strongly parabolic curve. When the regression analysis was converted to plot class interval on the x axis against frequency expressed logarithmically on the y axis as clear negative linear regression resulted. This regression formula is $y = ab^x$ where y = the frequency of linked units, x = the distance between linked units in feet, a = 64, and b = 2.71. The correlation coefficient for this regression is .873. This clearly indicates that broken pottery was not widely scattered at the site but tended to cluster about a single provenience unit; presumably the unit in which it was broken. As pottery tends to break in use this should indicate either the area of storage or the area in which it was last functionally employed.

It was clear from the sherd-linked unit analysis that the mean distance between sherds from a single vessel was 4.68 feet and that over 73% of all sherds from a single vessel were found less than 0.937 provenience units apart. Since the 74 provenience units on the site which were neither cultural features nor cut by the edge of the midden were all 5 × 5 foot squares, the maximum distance between two points within a single data set will be 7.0711 feet. This is greater than the mean values derived for sherd-linked units. It would seem, therefore, that the artificial segregation of ceramics by provenience units should not bias the correlations generated by the ISRMDC program. Nor do these correlations seem to be biased by the level of ceramic description employed. However, it is possible that recording attributes alone, rather than attribute clusters, would produce different correlations. Attribute clusters, however, are substantial while the pure attributes are analytic only. The level of ceramic analysis realized by the subvarietal groups seems to reflect sub-

stantive differences in this component. With these it is possible to create hypotheses concerning the relationships of ceramic decorations that reflect the shared experience of the potters. The subvarietal groups also reflect the functional differences in the ceramics as determined by vessel capacities.

In the analyses of the ceramics from the Middle Woodland level of the site, there was no significant degree of correlation observed between the mean vessel thickness and the mean rim diameter for all vessels within a single ceramic variety. This indicates that, within certain mechanical limits, vessel thickness is not determined by vessel size, and can probably be considered more of a stylistic than a functional variable.

Rim diameters were determined by comparing all rimsherds over 10 cm long from a single vessel to a sheet of cardboard inscribed with semi-circles of known diameter. The mean rim diameter for each vessel was thus determined. The mean rim diameter for the ceramic group was then computed from the mean vessel diameters. This method was used to avoid biasing the estimated rim diameter of the ceramic group by incorporating the extremes often found on individual sherds due to differential post-depositional warping as the result of earth pressures. The stated range of rim diameter for any ceramic group indicates the range for individual rimsherds, while the stated mean rim diameter is based on the described secondary vessel diameter (Table X).

While concepts of functionally differing ceramic groups of decoration are not generally utilized in this area of North America, some distinction can be made between ceremonial and utilitarian ceramic decorations in the Middle Woodland of Ohio, Illinois and adjacent areas (Griffin, 1965: 107-09). This fact should be kept in mind when comparing ceramics from a Minnesota burial mound to those recovered from a Michigan fishing village. Even within a single component of a non-ceremonial site variations in the uses of vessels may correlate with differing decorative elements. At the Late Woodland Spring Creek site in Muskegon Co., Michigan, Fitting (1968a: 22-29) has noted a highly significant association between rim type and rim diameter. This may be merely a mechanical

TABLE X  MEAN RIM DIAMETERS FOR MIDDLE WOODLAND VESSELS

| Ceramic Variety observed/expected | Class Limits For Rim Diameter | | | |
|---|---|---|---|---|
| | 15.0-22.0 cm | 22.1-28.0 cm | 28.1-35.0 cm | Total |
| Banked Stamp, Plain | 2/3.5 | 6/12.3 | 19/11.2 | 27 |
| Banked Stamp, Narrow | 2/2.4 | 15/8.6 | 2/8.0 | 19 |
| Plain, Unbossed, notched | 1/1.6 | 3/5.9 | 9/8.5 | 13 |
| Banked Stamp, Dentate | 3/1.6 | 9/5.9 | 1/8.5 | 13 |
| Dragged Stamp, Dentate | 1/1.5 | 2/5.5 | 1/8.5 | 12 |
| Dragged Stamp, Plain | 1/1.4 | 9/5.0 | 9/5.0 | 11 |
| Banked Punctage, Fingernail | 2/1.4 | 7/5.0 | 1/4.6 | 11 |
| Linear Stamped | 1/0.6 | 2/3.6 | 2/4.6 | 8 |
| Linear Incised, Interrupted | 1/0.9 | 2/3.2 | 3/2.9 | 7 |
| TOTAL | 15 | 55 | 51 | 121 |

$$\chi^2 \text{ with continuity correction} = 36.91$$
$$df = 16$$
$$p < .01$$
$$\phi 2 = 0.1757$$

Twelve vessels representing the three varieties; Linear Impressed Dentate Stamped, Miscellaneous Punctate, and Linear Incised simple criss-cross, could not be entered into this table due to expected cell frequencies of zero.

relationship due to the need for a thicker rim on larger vessels to prevent collapse during drying. In the Middle Woodland component at Summer Island, where there is also an association of certain decorations with vessels having a certain rim diameter (Table X), no such mechanical explanation can be invoked. Since the ratio of vessel height to rim diameter seems relatively constant and all vessels displayed a similar shape, three distinct size groupings for these vessels can be proposed. Using the volumetric formula for an eliptic paraboloid (Burlington, 1954) and the rim: height ratio observed on the reconstructed vessel (Plate V) (Brose, n.d.b), vessels having a rim diameter of about 20 cm will have a capacity of about 3.1 liters; vessels with a rim diameter of 25 cm will have a capacity of about 6 liters; and vessels with a rim diameter of 33 cm will have a capacity of just under 12 liters. If these three sizes of vessels represent functionally different uses of pottery, and as the designs applied to each different size group seem not to be random but rather culturally determined, functionally different areas of sites occupied by the same group during the course of a single seasonal cycle could be expected to show quite different frequencies of the various ceramic decorations.

*Sherd Weight.*—Because sherd size and mean sherd weight varied considerably across the site, numbers and weights of all ceramics recovered were recorded as separate variables within each data set. Following McPherron's hypothesis (1967: 254-55) that low mean sherd weights indicate areas of heavy foot traffic, an analysis of the areal distribution of mean sherd weight for each provenience unit was made. In Figure 9 each provenience unit in Area "C" illustrates the mean weight in grams of the sherds recovered from that unit. Comparison with Figures 3 and 8 clearly indicates that the lowest mean sherd weights occur in provenience units containing the inferred ($\bar{x} = 0.973$ grams). Units containing and surrounding hearths had a slightly higher mean sherd weight ($\bar{x} = 1.213$ grams), while units containing or surrounding the external subsidiary racks had a mean sherd weight of 1.455 grams. Those 5 × 5 foot squares containing the edges of the midden were entered as two separate data sets. In Figure 9 only that portion within the midden is represented. These units have a mean sherd weight of 1.875 grams. The mean sherd weight for units containing the external walls of the houses was 2.47 grams while the provenience units outside the midden producing Middle Woodland ceramics had a mean sherd weight of 3.192 grams.[3]

---

3. The inferred function of the structures seems supported by the application of McPherron's "trampling

(Continued on Page 49)

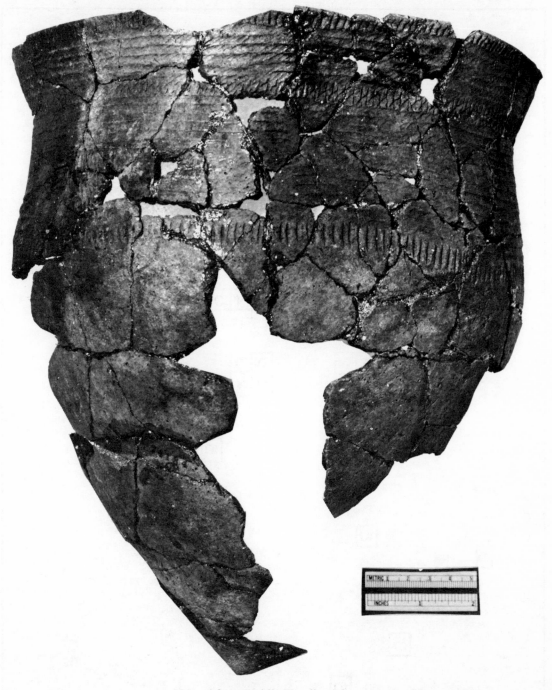

Plate V – Reconstructed Vessel from Middle Woodland Component of Summer Island

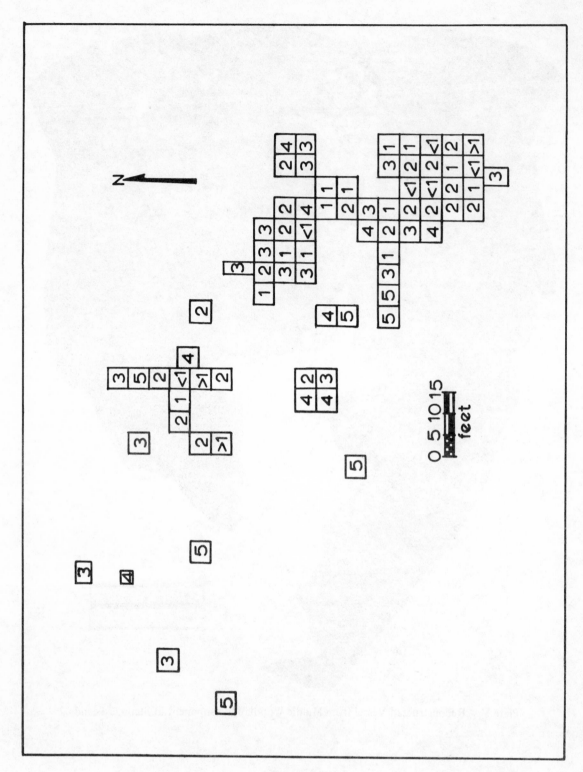

Figure 9

With reference to the McPherron trampling index, it is quite interesting to note that the central or southwestern Area "C" showed no midden accumulation although it had the highest mean sherd weights for the entire site. Most traffic seems to have passed on the lakeward side of the arc of structures, the only exceptions being ancillary structures $I_B$ and $II_B$ located just to the west of the houses. To some extent the lack of any area located at the center of the habitational arc is unusual. On further reflection it is not too surprising. The dependence of this component of the site on the lake, both for subsistence and communication, would not require either extensive or intensive traffic from the houses inland. The major faunal resource, fish, does not require the type of central cooking area noted for some peoples in the Great Lakes whose economy apparently focused on big game hunting (Fitting, Devisscher, and Wahla, 1966). As a further note, it might be added that in trudging about on sand dunes one prefers to stay where vegetation to some degree stabilizes the dune, or on the well-trodden path if one exists. The relatively small areas of extra-dwelling traffic, as seen in mean sherd weights, are not at all unreasonable in view of the nature of the occupation.

*Statistical Analyses.*—Given the relatively homogeneous nature of the ceramics recovered in the Middle Woodland component and the short period of occupation, it was clear that the decorative differences within the ceramics could not be due to temporal change. Although some of the styles might be coming into favor while others were losing popularity, if this were the only factor involved, the areal distribution of different ceramic decorations should be completely random across the component. To

---

(Continued from Page 46)
index." To test the possibility that the observed variance in sherd weights may have been a function of ceramic type rather than sherd volume, a random sample of four sherds of each ceramic variety were tested for specific gravity. The results of these tests indicated that specific gravity for all types varied between 2.5 and 2.9 with no significant correlations between ceramic types and the weight of sherds of equal volume. Mean sherd weight differences clearly represent differential degrees of breakage and the McPherron trampling index does serve to determine traffic patterns at the site.

test this possibility, the mean vessel occurrence per type for each individual provenience unit was used to compute a Poisson distribution of expected frequency of any decorative ceramic group in all provenience units. The actual distribution was compared to this and the significance of the differences was tested by a Chi square test. The results of these tests indicated that the observed distributions were not random. Significant differences existed with respect to the distribution of different ceramic varieties among different provenience units within the component. Since all areas of the component were simultaneously occupied, some factor related to the area on the site must have been responsible for the differential distribution of ceramic decoration.

One possibility which would account for the differential distribution of ceramic decoration would be a functional relationship between the area of the component and the ceramics. In Table X, certain functional differences (expressed as vessel size) could clearly be seen to correlate with ceramic decoration. One class of vessels having a capacity of just over three liters tended to be decorated as Linear Impressed, Dentate Stamp; Banked Stamp, Narrow tool variety (horizontal); or Banked Punctate, Fingernail variety. Vessels having a capacity of about six liters tended to be decorated as Dragged Stamp, Plain tool; Banked Stamp, Dentate tool; Banked Stamp, Narrow tool (oblique); Linear Incised (criss-cross); or Banked Punctate, Fingernail variety. Vessels with a capacity of just under twelve liters tended to be decorated as Dragged Stamp, Dentate tool; Banked Stamp, Plain tool (oblique); Banked Stamp, Plain tool (chevron); or Linear Impressed, Corded stamp variety. The Plain, unbossed, notched lip ceramics and the Linear Incised, Interrupted variety ceramics seemed to display a random distribution for vessel size.

While these associations were not invariable neither were they random. They could be expected to occur by chance alone (sampling error) less than once in a hundred cases. The association of these differences in plastic decoration with vessels of different sizes is not a mechanical one. There is nothing inherent in the size of the vessel which determines what type of decoration it will bear. While the areal distribution of ceramic decoration within this component will certainly be affected by the differing uses to which the different sized vessels were put, it cannot be explained by this alone.

Through a second modification of the computer program, it was possible to perform systematic regression analyses for the frequencies of vessels of each ceramic variety against all other varieties, singlely or in combination. Product-moment correlation coefficients were computed for these regressions. The correlation coefficients are presented in matrix form in Table XI.[4]

It is apparent from Table XI that while most varieties show no significant correlations there are a number of ceramic varieties which correlate quite highly with one another ($a$ = .001) and still other ceramic varieties which correlate with somewhat less certainty ($a$ = .05). Following the method employed by Freeman and

## TABLE XI CORRELATION COEFFICIENT MATRIX: MIDDLE WOODLAND CERAMICS
### (FOR VARIABLE NUMBER SEE TABLE VI)

| | | 41 | 42 | 46 | 47 | 71 | 72 | 73 | 74 | 75 | 76 | 77 | 78 |
|---|---|---|---|---|---|---|---|---|---|---|---|---|---|
| **42** | r | -.027 | | | | | | | | | | | |
| | a | | | | | | | | | | | | |
| **46** | r | -.006 | .027 | | | | | | | | | | |
| | a | | | | | | | | | | | | |
| **47** | r | -.014 | .106 | .182 | | | | | | | | | |
| | a | | | .05 | | | | | | | | | |
| **71** | r | .931 | -.040 | .027 | .052 | | | | | | | | |
| | a | .001 | | | | | | | | | | | |
| **72** | r | -.020 | -.003 | .014 | -.030 | -.017 | | | | | | | |
| | a | | | | | | | | | | | | |
| **73** | r | -.023 | .077 | .004 | -.002 | -.023 | .318 | | | | | | |
| | a | | | | | | .05 | | | | | | |
| **74** | r | -.041 | .081 | -.049 | .079 | -.014 | .010 | .025 | | | | | |
| | a | | | | | | | | | | | | |
| **75** | r | .025 | .010 | -.022 | -.022 | .102 | -.033 | .006 | .806 | | | | |
| | a | | | | | | | | .001 | | | | |
| **76** | r | .011 | .141 | .148 | -.282 | .143 | .038 | .063 | -.183 | .442 | | | |
| | a | | | | .05 | | | | | .02 | | | |
| **77** | r | .080 | .043 | .167 | -.068 | .158 | -.034 | -.061 | .712 | .834 | .502 | | |
| | a | | | .05 | | | | | | .001 | .01 | | |
| **78** | r | .026 | .007 | .046 | .080 | .113 | -.026 | .054 | .774 | .873 | .632 | .823 | |
| | a | | | | | | | | .001 | .001 | .01 | .001 | |
| **79** | r | -.027 | .097 | .037 | -.018 | .27 | -.044 | -.075 | .748 | .894 | .450 | .862 | .820 |
| | a | | | | | | | | .001 | .001 | .02 | .001 | .001 |

4. The value of r is an indication of the accuracy with which the value of one variable can be determined from knowledge of the other variable; that is, it is an indication of how similar the two variables are in their behavior in each and all of the 134 provenience units within the component. Where $r = 0$, no prediction is possible. A perfect correlation is represented by $r = +1$ or $r = -1$: the positive correlation indicates that as the frequency of one variable increases the frequency of the second variable also increases correspondingly. The negative correlation indicates that as the frequency of one variable increases the frequency of the other variable decreases correspondingly. A perfect negative correlation would indicate the replacement of one variable by the other. The $a$ value was determined by a single-tailed F-test and by comparison to levels of significance for the distribution of "F" (Blalock, 1960: 248). In the matrix (Table XI), only those cells where $a$ .05 are filled, lower values being considered the result of sampling error.

Brown (1964: 128-130), it is possible to recognize six constellations of Middle Woodland ceramic varieties from the Summer Island site, showing mutual positive correlation coefficients. These constellations described by their machine coded variable numbers were as follows:

A) 41, 71 ($a$ = .001)
B) 72, 73 ($a$ = .05)
C) 46, 47, 76 ($a$ = .05)
D) 46, 77 ($a$ = .05)
E) 74, 75, 77, 78, 79 ($a$ = .001)
F) 75, 76, 77, 78, 79 ($a$ = .001)

To quote Freeman and Brown, describing the Carter Ranch ceramics,

> These groups of types are mutually exclusive and exhaustive on the basis of the correlations. In other words, when types 1 and 3 correlate with each other and with (type) 4, and when type 2 likewise correlates with (types) 3 and 4 but not with (type) 1, two such groups of types are established: 1, 3, 4 and 2, 3, 4.
>
> We therefore postulate . . . that there are four constellations of pottery types at the Carter Ranch which either were temporally or 'functionally' different, or both . . . [*idem*: p. 129-30].

Since these constellations at Summer Island are found at a site of limited duration, significant changes in ceramic styles would not be expected. Furthermore, any changes in stylistic popularity could be expected to have random distribution. This is not the case as has been noted above.

While admitting that the bases of these constellations cannot be elucidated from the coefficients alone, Freeman and Brown make it clear that they consider functional differences paramount (*idem:* p. 126, 130-31, 134, 139). If the differences in vessel function as inferred by capacity are used as a criterion for classification the breakdown for the varieties of ceramic decoration, using the machine coded variable numbers, would be:

> Large:    41, 42, 46, 71, 74, 76
> Medium:  42, 47, 71, 73, 75, 77
> Small:    42, 71, 72, 77, 79

Comparing the above groupings to the ceramic constellations generated by mutual correlations indicates that functional explanations are insufficient. Constellation A consists of one large and one medium subvariety. Constellation B consists of one medium and a small subvariety. Constellation C consists of two large and one medium subvariety. Constellations E and F both consist of one large, three medium, and one small subvariety.

These ceramic constellations do not always correlate with specific functional areas of the site insofar as can be determined. Most of the individual subvarieties of decoration show rather definite areas of occurrence on the site. Linear Impressed, Corded Stamped sherds (variable 41) occurred in the entrance to Structure I; at the northern hearth (Feature 12) along the northwest wall, and at Feature 4 within Structure I; at ancillary Structure $I_B$; and in the hearth within Structure II (Feature 20). Linear Incised, Interrupted variety (variable 42) occurred in the western and eastern hearths in Structure III; in units associated with Structure IV; and at ancillary structures $I_A$, $I_B$, and $II_B$. Dragged Stamp, Plain tool variety (variable 47) occurs along the walls outside the eastern half of Structure I; at the eastern hearth in Structure III; and at ancillary Structures $I_A$, $I_B$, $II_A$, and $III_A$. Dragged Stamp, Dentate tool variety (variable 46) occurred in the entrance and along the eastern wall within Structure I; at the southern hearth (Feature 45) and at Feature 46 within this structure; at Feature 39; in the western portion of Structure III just north of the hearth (Feature 40); and at ancillary Structure $II_A$. Plain, unbossed, notched lip sherds (variable 71) occurred at the entrance to Structure III; at the entrance and just north of the hearth within Structure II; at the entrance and at the southern hearth (Feature 45) and northern hearth (Feature 12) in Structure I; and at ancillary Structure $I_B$ and $II_A$. Linear Impressed, Dentate Stamped sherds (variable 72) occurred in Structure I along the west wall; associated with the northern hearth (Feature 45); and just to the north of the southern hearth (Feature 45); as well as in units associated with Structure IV. Linear Incised, uniform variety (criss-cross) (variable 73) occurred outside the entrance to Structure III; in units associated with Structure IV; at the entrance and just to the east of the southern hearth in Structure I; and at ancillary Structures $I_A$ and $III_A$. Banked Stamp, Plain tool variety (chevron) (variable 74) occurred in the entrance and southeast of the southern hearth (Feature 45) in

Structure I; just south of the hearth within Structure II; at the entrance to Structure III; and at ancillary Structures I$_B$, and III$_A$. Banked Stamp, Dentate tool (variable 75) sherds occurred within and to the west of the western hearth in Structure III; and outside the entrance; to the west of the northern hearth (Feature 12) within Structure I as well as in the entrance; and at ancillary Structures I$_B$, II$_A$, II$_B$, and III$_A$. Banked Stamp, Plain tool variety (oblique) (variable 76) occurred within the northern hearth and along the east wall within Structure I as well as in the entrance; in the entrance and at the western hearth in Structure III; in units associated with Structure IV; and at ancillary Structures I$_A$ and II$_B$. Banked Punctate, Fingernail sherds (variable 77) occurred within and just to the west of the entrance in Structure I as well as just to the southeast of the southern hearth (Feature 45); along the northern part of the northern hearth and the western wall in Structure I; and at ancillary Structures I$_A$, I$_B$, II$_A$, and II$_B$. Banked Stamp, Narrow tool (oblique) sherds (variable 78) occurred at both hearths and in the entrance to Structure I; along the west wall within the same structure; and at ancillary Structures I$_A$, I$_B$, II$_A$, and II$_B$. Banked Stamp Narrow tool (horizontal) (variable 79) sherds occurred at almost all areas within Structure II and at all ancillary structures. Nearly all of the Miscellaneous Punctate sherds (variable 45) were recovered from units associated with Structures III and IV or from ancillary Structures I$_B$, II$_A$, and III$_A$.

*Functional Interpretations.*—While several of the ceramic constellations do show their highest co-occurrence at rather restricted, functionally specific areas of the site, others do not. It seems more rewarding to interpret each constellation individually rather than look for a single all-encompassing explanation. Before any functional interpretation is offered for any of the ceramic constellations a summary statement can be made regarding the locations of the site where the co-occurrence of their constituent ceramic varieties are found. Constellation A occurred outside the entrance to Structures I and III; at the hearth within Structure II; and at ancillary Structure I$_B$. Constellation B occurred at Structure IV, and at the south hearth within Structure I. Constellation C occurred in eastern Structure III and at ancillary Structure II$_A$. Constellation D occurred at ancillary Structure II$_A$ and at the southern hearth in Structure I. Constellation E occurred at ancillary Structures I$_B$ and III$_A$ while Constellation F occurred at ancillary Structures I$_A$, II$_A$, and II$_B$.

Ancillary Structures I$_A$, II$_A$, and III$_A$ were all interpreted as fish drying racks and they would seem to be functional equivalents. This is also true for ancillary Structures I$_B$ and II$_B$, both of which were interpreted as predominantly meat drying racks. Since constellations E and F are found in association with these structures, a strong case can be made for regarding them as functionally equivalent also.

The only difference between these constellations is the replacement of Banked Stamp, Plain tool (chevron) in the former by Banked Stamp, Plain tool (oblique) in the latter. Both of these ceramic variants tend to be large vessels and might be considered to be in free variation functionally. However, the only significant negative correlation from the entire component was that observed between these two ceramic decorations. The only provenience units in which these ceramics mutually occur were in the entrance to Structure III, in an exterior refuse pit (Feature 5), and a few scattered sherds at ancillary Structures I$_B$ and III$_A$. If the basis of Constellations E and F is functional, the difference between them cannot be.

Furthermore, Banked Stamp Plain tool (oblique) variant is the most popular decoration within the component (Table 4). If it is so poorly represented in areas of the site which are functionally equivalent to those areas where it occurs in high numbers, the explanation can not be functional one. Vessels of this popular ceramic style were abundant within Structures III and IV and from the northern hearth within Structure I. These are the areas where its functional equivalent, Banked Stamp, Plain tool (chevron) was totally absent. This latter variety was strongly represented at the other two interior hearths however, while at these areas the oblique variety was conspicuously absent. Since these fireplaces within the houses are more intimately associated with a limited and relatively constant group of individuals, the assumption is made that the replacement of functionally equivalent vessels is dictated by the personal preferences of those individuals involved.

For the other ceramic constellations certain hearth areas also seem to be associated. Structure

IV clearly can be seen as the focus for Constellation B, although these ceramics also occur together at the southern hearth in **Structure I**. The eastern hearth in **Structure III** shows a preference for Constellation C. Structure II shows a strong preference for Constellation A, although these ceramics also occur at the northern hearth in **Structure I**. This southern hearth in **Structure I** is the only hearth where Constellation D occurs. Since all these hearths are assumed to have served a similar function, the differences in their associated ceramic constellations are assumed to be stylistic rather than functional.

A detailed analysis of the function of each ceramic constellation is not really possible. To some extent each constellation incorporates several different sizes of vessels. All vessels with the exception of those of the two Banked Stamp Plain tool varieties showed large areas of burnt food remains above the shoulder, indicating that these pots had been used for cooking. While the lack of such deposits is not conclusive, it might be an indication that these two varieties of large vessels were used primarily for storage. While every hearth seems to have had a different number of ceramic variants all had a similar ratio of vessel size.

Within the structures no clear association between types of ceramic decoration or size and faunal remains was observed. If the ancillary structures have been correctly interpreted, then there are only three ceramic decorations which show any constant correlation with faunal remains. The large vessels of Linear Impressed, Braided Cord stamped variety occurred only at meat drying racks. The small Linear Incised, Interrupted variety occurred only with fish remains. And the medium-sized Linear Incised, Uniform variety (criss-cross) never occurred with any faunal remains. All other varieties appear to have been less functionally specialized.

*Stylistic Analyses.*—A much better understanding of the areal distribution of the ceramic varieties is obtained when these are considered as culturally determined stylistic variations within each size class. Several facts are immediately apparent. No use of the dragged-stamp technique occurred at **Structure IV**. No use of a dentate tool occurred at **Structure II**. The two large ceramic constellations, E and F, are composed solely of variations of the Banked Stamp decora-

tion. At **Structure I** dragged-stamp decorated ceramics occurred at the southern hearth only. The only use of Fingernail Punctate ceramics occurred at this hearth and in **Structure II**. From a review of the ethnographic data it is clear that intra-house fireplaces are used by a **single** nuclear family. It is also clear that the ceramics used by each of these families are generally those produced by the women of that family. While some aboriginal exchange may have occurred at this time level, the major items exchanged could be expected to be food stuffs. While some of these items were undoubtedly contained in ceramic vessels, this exchange was primarily across ecological boundaries (see G. Wright, 1967) and the ceramics from these other areas should be quite distinct from the local wares (e.g., Mason, 1967: 298-99; Plate 11). There is no evidence for any area specializing in the manufacture of pottery for exchange such as reported from the New Guinea mainland (Harding, 1967: 36-38). Even there, within the local area, exchange of ceramics moves along kinship lines (*idem*: p. 90, 106).

Several recent archaeological studies have indicated that within a site representing occupation by a group whose level of social organization is no more complex than tribal, the distribution of design elements on ceramics can be used to infer the distribution of women who have shared the ceramic learning experience (Deetz, 1965: 2, 96-102; Longacre, 1964: 155-158, 166-167). In Deetz's example, the Medicine Crow Site was known to have been occupied by a group whose social organization was changing from matrilocal, matrilineal to one less rigidly matrilocal. Deetz was able to demonstrate an increasingly random association of ceramic attributes over the period of time represented at the site. This he inferred from the assumption that,

> if culturally conditioned behavioral patterning is responsible for artifactual patterning, then changes in the . . . behavioral patterning . . . affect the attribute patterning seen in the resulting objects. A connection between social structure and ceramics might be seen in the possible changes in design configurations in ceramics as they reflect a change in the residence rule of the culture which produced them [*op. cit.* :2] .

Longacre's study of the ceramics from the Carter Ranch Site was an attempt to "... define geographical clusterings of (ceramic design) elements and then to correlate these with kinship groupings as suggested from the ethnography of the Western Pueblos." (*op. cit.*: 157). Longacre based his analysis on the hypothesis that

> social demography and social organization are reflected in the material cultural system. In a matrilineal, matrilocal society, social demography may be mirrored in the ceramic art of female potters; the smaller and more closely tied the social aggregate, the more details of design would be shared. Augumented by clues from other aspects of the cultural system, differential relative frequencies of elements of design may suggest the delimitation of various social aggregates: (1), (2) *[sic]* larger social units such as the villages interacting in a relatively large area and producing pottery of the same variety or type, (3) groups of villages forming a unit through social interaction along kin-based, religious, and political lines, (4) the village as a social group, and (5) localized matrilineages or lineage segments forming a village. (*op. cit.*: 158).[5]

Both studies, although archaeological reports, have worked from known or assumed ethnographic data to interpret the distribution of archaeological materials. Both are based on a premise of matrilocal residence producing clusters of attributes or high frequencies of a particular design element. At Summer Island no such approach is possible. The social demography of the inhabitants is quite unknown and ethnographic assumptions would be rash. It is not at all certain that from archaeological data alone that demographic reconstructions can be made which will preclude differing reconstructions from being applicable. While agreeing with Deetz and Longacre that the horizontal distribution of ceramic design attributes within the component represents the residential patterning of the women who used and presumably made those ceramics, one must be cognizant of factors which will tend to destroy the clear correlations which the assumed data alone would produce. As Longacre noted (*op. cit.*: 166), there are design elements which will probably be employed by all of the female potters within the village. At Summer Island the use of a plain tool to form the Banked Stamp motif would be an example of this tendency.

Somewhat more sensitive to areal change was the angle at which these stamped designs were applied, all being uniformly oblique at Features 12, 31, 40, and in Structure IV, and all being alternately oblique (chevron) at Features 20 and 45. If the ceramics associated with these hearths can be assumed to represent those designs employed by the women of that family

---

5. In both of these studies, several methodological weaknesses occur. Deetz deals with each chronologically sequent component as a single data set, giving no distribution for materials within the component. Deetz also considers attributes such as vessel profile and location and type of handles comparable to attributes such as location of decoration or lip design elements (*op. cit.*: 47-48). These attributes are not of equal stylistic significance: the former examples may well be associated with vessel function while the latter are not. Finally, while some degree of bimodality (indicative of non-random attribute association) can be seen in most of the histograms for the earliest component, some degree also occurs in most of the histograms relating to the latest component and the greatest degree of bimodality generally can be found in histograms relating to the intermediate component. While the comparison of cumulative histograms for all three components definitely supports Deetz's conclusions, analysis of any single component along the methodological lines he has used would be quite inconclusive in attempting to determine the significance of the association of attributes.

Longacre's study was based on a selected sample of potsherds from the Carter Ranch site wherein only a single variety was utilized to determine the inter-village distribution of design elements (*op. cit.*: 162). To the extent that the village clearly represents a close social aggregate, Longacre had earlier hypothesized that a large number of types and varieties should not occur (*loc. cit.*). Some qualitative description of these extraneous sherds should have been given, and the reasons for their rejection stated. The use of similar frequencies of similar design elements on distinct types of varieties of ceramics is used to infer a "valley tradition" (*op. cit.*: 167), although the rationale for this inference is not clear. Finally, only forty percent of the design elements displayed non-random distribution and only nine (5.1 percent) of the design elements were considered sensitive for illustrating the social demography (*idem*: Figs. 65-57). This leads to the speculation that much of the areal distribution may have been rather random after all.

in the production of ceramics, each of the six families (represented by the five hearths and Structure IV) can be assigned the following repetoire of designs (see Table V for type-variety machine code):

Structure I, south hearth; Variables 46, 71, 72, 73, 74, 77, 78.

Structure I, north hearth: Variables 41, 71, 72, 75, 76, 77, 78.

Structure II: Variables 41, 71, 74, 79.

Structure III, southeast hearth; Variables 42, 45, 47.

Structure III, northwest hearth; Variables 42, 45, 46, 75, 76.

Structure IV; Variables 42, 45, 72, 73, 76.

If the results of the studies by Deetz and Longacre are valid, then the residence patterns displayed by the ceramics at Summer Island argue against a matrilocal, matrilineal social organization. Greater differences exist between the ceramics at the two hearths within Structure III than exist between the northwest hearth and Structure IV. Between the two hearths in Structure I less than 50% of the ceramic designs are shared and these are the most common ones at the site. If the women at Structures I or III were matrilineal relatives, they would both have had the same ceramic learning experiences and could be expected to share most of their designs. A basic technique such as dragged stamping would not be expected to occur only at one hearth within both of these structures and not at the other. If the residence pattern favored matrilocality, regardless of the system of descent reckoning, the two hearths within each structure should be occupied either by a mother and daughter or by two sisters and should show a greater sharing of ceramic design than is in fact observed (see Deetz, 1965: 93-96).

If the residence patterns at Summer Island favored patrilocality or bilocality a different distribution of ceramic design could be expected. Bilocal residence would allow the expectation that of the six families at Summer Island at least one might be the result of post-nuptial matrilocal residence. If this had in fact occurred, two of the six hearths from the component should be rather close in their ceramic decoration. Ceramically the closest group consists of the two hearths within Structure I. The reasons against regarding this as a matrilocal residence have already been pre-sented. If bilocal residence was the preferred pattern at Summer Island it would seem that all post-nuptial residence upon the island had, in fact, been patrilocal. The presence of two structures containing multiple hearths with significantly different ceramic design as-sembledges argues against a practice of neolocal residence.

The only other post-nuptial residence pattern remaining is one of preferred patri-locality. This may have been a rather strongly followed pattern, or it may merely be a result of a particular sample within a group practicing a bilocal pattern.

Deetz (1965: 95) has argued that patri-locality, "... expectably should produce no patterning of design elements in the case of female ceramic manufacture ... [there is no] ... influence which could be thought of as aiding in the preservation of design configura-tions to any significant extent whatsoever." Deetz referred to the situation where

> ... under a patrilocal rule of resi-dence when a young girl reached an age at which skills such as the manufacture of pottery would be acquired, they would be taught to her by her paternal grandmother, who in turn had learned the art from her paternal grandmother, resulting in an alternation of designs totally unlike the linear transmission thought to be character-istic of the matricentered pattern, [op. cit.: 97-98].

While a pattern of paternal grandmother-young girl instruction need not be assumed for Summer Island it is ethnographically well-reported from the area (Hilger, 1951: 56-57). In either case, whether mother or grandmother was the in-structress, Deetz has indicated that a random distribution of ceramic design is expectable with patrilocal residence.

As demonstrated both by the ceramic con-stellations generated from the correlation co-efficient matrix and by the distribution of ceramic designs associated with the family hearths, the areal distribution of ceramics at Summer Island is not random. The occurrence of ceramic Constellation A at the north hearth in Structure I and the hearth in Structure II, the occurrence of Constellation B with Structure IV and the south hearth in Structure I, the consistant negative correlations between variable 74 and 76 at all hearths, and the fact that those hearths in Structure I are closest in distance as well as ceramically closest, all are evidence for some degree of culturally patterned behavior.

appear to be as close as to the female at the south hearth. This may be a result of sampling error, for if vessels of Linear Impressed Dentate stamp (variable 72) were recovered from subsequent work in the little excavated western

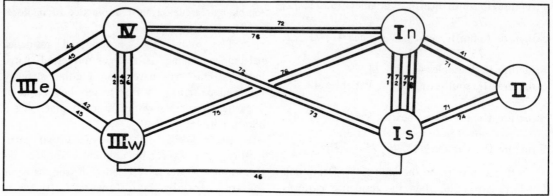

Figure 10

The number of shared ceramic designs can be taken as a measure (to some degree) of shared ceramic learning experience between the females. Some indication of these patterns can be seen in Figure 10 where the number of shared designs is illustrated by the number of lines connecting the respective hearth areas (indicated by circles). Two clusters can be seen, one defined by variables 42 and 45, and the other by variable 71.

Several explanations can be offered for these patterns. If the sharing of designs indicates these females are related through a paternal relative (since with patrilocality their maternal relatives would have had a different residence), the females at the two hearths within Structure I, as well as the women from Structure IV and the western hearth in Structure III are seen to be closely related. The female in Structure II is certainly related to the Structure I females, if to no others on the site, although this relationship is not as close as that between the two females within Structure I. There are also probable relationships between the female at the eastern hearth within Structure III and females from the western hearth in Structure III and from Structure IV. Some degree of shared design exists between these two rather clear clusters. A possible relationship exists between the female at Structure IV and both females within Structure I. The female at the western hearth within Structure III is also related to both women from Structure I, although the relationship does not

portion of Structure III, the schematic diagram (Figure 10) would be perfectly symmetrical. Its close approach to symmetry is further argument against the ceramic designs being randomly distributed.

While there is little reasonable doubt concerning the closeness of male relatives sharing a single house in a society apparently practicing bilocal or patrilocal residence, the exact nature of that relationship cannot be determined with certainty. If the males within Structure I were married to women who are in fact sisters, it would be more reasonable to suppose the male relationship was between two brothers rather than between father and son. At Summer Island, where apparently both males have married women sharing their basic ceramic learning experience but not the entire design repetoire (as would be expected between sisters), some rather interesting speculations can be raised to account for the observed ceramic design distributions.

Granted Deetz's stipulation that in patrilocal societies the paternal grandmother is the person from whom a young girl will probably learn ceramic design, a random distribution of these designs would occur only if preferred marriage patterns were also random. The distribution observed at Summer Island is not consistant with such a pattern. Given a small patrilocal group, whether band or tribal segment, some form of reciprocal band exogamy or lineage exogamy could be predicted (Service,

1962: 66-67; Sahlins, 1968: 56-63). Also expectable would be some preferential form of marital alliance, normally a type of cross-cousin marriage (Service, *loc. cit.*; Sahlins, 1968: 58-59) such as characterized the Indians of the thinly populated upper Great Lakes prior to acculturation (Eggan, 1966: 78-111; Callender, 1962; Hickerson, 1962).[6]

If the preferred pattern is for patrilateral cross-cousin marriage, it becomes important whether the mother or the grandmother instructs the young girl in making ceramics, and it will also matter how many lineages or bands are represented in the network of marriage alliances. On the one hand, if the mother instructs the girl, no matter how many lineages or bands are inter-marrying, a man and his son will always marry women of different ceramic groups. On the other hand, if the paternal grandmother instructs the young girl an interesting pattern emerges. In Figure 11, a patrilateral cross-cousin marriage pattern is diagrammed for a society having three distinct ceramic design clusters (indicated in Figure 11 by the three different female-symbol shadings), each originating with a separate lineage or band within the marriage network and passing

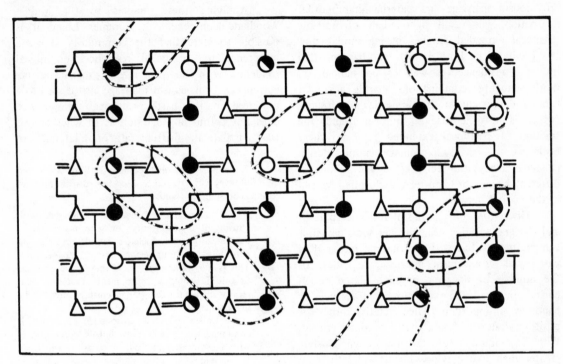

Figure 11

6. Callender (personal communication) has commented on this interpretation of the Summer Island archaeological data:

> As for marriage, my own argument for the Proto-Central Algonquian postulated the bilateral cross-cousin form, mostly because this is the type found among those Naskapi, Salteaux, etc. who were still practicing cross-cousin marriage when they were described ... these are invariably the more northern groups, whose terminology differs from both PCA and contemporary Ojibwa. My earlier interpretation attributed this to a more consistent practice of bilateral cross-cousin marriage, but possibly it can be explained through a shift from some other, narrower form

> to the bilateral kind. Hockett argues for matri-lateral cross-cousin marriage and patrilocal residence, his hypothesis being based entirely on terminological correspondences. Eggan notes Hockett's position, but seems to reserve judgment, because only the bilateral variety has been reported. Hickerson is strongly opposed to Hockett. The trouble with patrilateral xcm is that it seems a rather rare type of marriage system in itself, the further problem being that it's so surrounded by acrimonious controversy that a clear view may be impossible to obtain. And I have an idea that it is usually (not inevitably) supposed to accompany matrilineal descent.

to a young girl from her paternal grandmother. Of all possible **patrilocal** extended households composed of a man and his son, two-thirds will show two different ceramic design clusters (indicated in Figure 11 by enclosured within a dot-and-dashed line), while one-third (indicated by enclosure within a lighter broken line) will display two similar ceramic design clusters. Within one-third of the nuclear families mother and daughter will also share the same ceramic design cluster. The similarity of these fractions is not merely coincidental. Where only two different ceramic design clusters are posited, patrilateral cross-cousin marriage and paternal grandmother instruction will result in one-half of possible patrilocal extended families having similar clusters produced by both women who have married into the residence, as well as one-half of all mother-daughter combinations sharing a similar ceramic design cluster. If sample size is sufficient (which is not the case at Summer Island) the fraction of patrilocal extended families where both women share a similar ceramic design cluster is always the reciprocal of the number of different lineage or band related clusters involved in the marital network.

Given the same patrilocal residence pattern and the grandmother teaching her son's daughter ceramic design, but with matrilateral rather than patrilateral cross-cousin marriage, regardless of the number of lineage— or band-related design clusters involved, the exact number of lineages or bands is unimportant. Their relative order or position along the "flow chart" becomes crucial. With any number of ceramic design clusters greater than two it is possible to order these so that either one-half of all patrilocal extended families will contain two women who have married into the residence and who share the same design repetoire, or none will. This will also be true for mother-daughter sharing of ceramic design clusters. If the ceramic design tradition passes directly from mother to daughter rather than from the paternal grandmother, matrilateral cross-cousin marriage will never result in two women sharing the same ceramic design cluster marrying into the same patrilocal extended family.

Contrary to what Deetz has stated (*loc. cit.*), patrilocal residence without direct mother-daughter ceramic design continuity produces rather significant patterning of ceramic design

elements. With statistically adequate samples it may be possible to recognize a preference for cross-cousin marriage and in some cases to determine whether it was patrilateral or matrilateral. The degree to which the exogamous community articulated with similar patrilocal groups could also be inferred (where patrilateral cross-cousin marriage can be demonstrated) from the reciprocal relationship seen to exist between the number of extended patrilocal families with female affines who share a ceramic design cluster and the number of such ceramic design clusters forming the marital network.

Applying these models to the Middle Woodland component at Summer Island it is possible to state that the community shows a preference for patrilocal residence (or bilocal residence with no recognizable matrilocal occurrences). Cross-cousin marriage also is seen as a preferred marital pattern although sample size does not permit any decision as to whether this was patrilateral, matrilateral, or bilateral.[7] In

---

7. Despres (personal communication) has noted the following in reference to the distribution of ceramics at Summer Island:

When bilateral exchange is combined with patrilocality-matrilineality; or with matrilocality-patrilineality; such societies can dichotomize indefinitely into four, eight, sixteen, etc. sections. This is the Kariera system. If there were evidence of this, it would seem to me that at least four clearly distinguishable design clusters ought to be in evidence.

Unless bilateral cross-cousin marriage is combined with patrilocality and matrilineality; or with matrilocality and patrilineality; it will force the development of a moiety system. In other words, if the rule of descent is consistent with the rule of residence, and if the rule of marriage is bilateral, then a society must be split in two groups (which may be lineages or combinations thereof) and only two design clusters should be evident. Furthermore, the possibility of extending such a network to incorporate more than the two groups seems extremely limited.

If you have patrilineality with patrilocal residence and at least three design clusters, then it seems to me that bilateral exchange is not possible. However, patrilateral or matrilateral exchange should be possible. I would argue against the first not only because it is rare but also because it does not seem capable of attaining any other form than a multitude of little closed systems, juxtaposed to one another, without ever realizing a "global" structure.    In other

either case the ceramic design clusters were probably taught to the young girl by her father's mother rather than her own mother. If the marriage pattern was preferential patrilateral cross-cousin marriage (such as might be expected of a unilineal descent group organized to exploit a fishing area collectively and cooperatively (see Hickerson, 1960; 1967: 327)), the two women in **Structure I** would probably have the relationship of MoBrWi-HuSiDa while if the preferred pattern were matrilateral cross-cousin marriage (such as Callender (1962) and Hockett (1964: 765) have proposed for the Proto-Central Algonkian Indians) these two women would have a FaSi-BrDa relationship.

The relationship of the women within **Structure III** would presumably be the same as those in **Structure I** unless bilateral cross-cousin marriage was practiced. The fact that the former two women do not show the same strength of relationship is no argument against this model for with either type of cross-cousin marriage, in at least half of the cases the women within patri-local extended house-holds would not show shared ceramic design clusters.

It may, of course, be the case that this model, for all its applicability, does not represent the situation at the Middle Woodland component on Summer Island. The sharing of ceramic design may merely indicate that the women from nearby structures made their pottery together (noted as a possible explanation for the functional interpretation of Feature 39) and borrowed ideas from each other on the island rather

than sharing a ceramic learning experience as children or receiving instruction from related females. Ethnographic examples of this group production by women are well-documented (e.g., Bunzel, 1929: 63-64; Hilger, 1951: 55-58, 109, 130-37; Speck, 1947: 11). However, in all such cases considerable acculturative processes were also at work. Even in these cases the work parties were generally organized along kinship lines (Bunzel, *loc. cit.*; Hilger, *loc. cit.*; Speck, *op. cit.*: 15, 25). If the women at Summer Island were not, in fact kin, their common residence and shared experience might have made them appear related both to any outside observer, and perhaps in time, to themselves also (Titiev, 1943: 515-530).

## CHIPPED STONE AND BONE

*Introduction.*—The analysis of areal distributions for the chipped stone and bone materials recovered from the Middle Woodland component at Summer Island does not yield results comparable to the analysis of ceramic styles. For the ceramics, stylization can to a great degree be divorced from function, while with stone and bone tools the media are not capable of carrying any but the bare functional forms. For this reason the functional interpretation of these distributions is far clearer than that of the ceramics and little data concerning social organization is directly generated.

*Statistical Analyses.*—By entering all artifacts as linear variables a product-moment correlation coefficient matrix was derived for all data sets pertaining to the Middle Woodland occupation of the site. A portion of this matrix is presented as Table XII with only those correlations significant at the probability level of >.05 represented. From this matrix it is possible to derive 26 constellations which were mutually exclusive and exhaustive on the basis of the correlations. These constellations represent artifacts and faunal remains which relate in a similar fashion within the excavation units and features of this component in much the same manner as the ceramic constellations described above. A listing of the variables forming each of these constellations is presented below:

A:     26, 27, 28, 62, 63, 64
B:     26, 27, 28, 49, 51

---

words, patrilateral exchange in either a matrilineal or a patrilineal society tends to be extremely restrictive in terms of the ecological permutation of exchange networks. Thus, in association with such a pattern, you should expect to find three or more ceramic design clusters but such clusters ought to be highly differentiated from neighboring areas.

Thus, assuming you have three or more design clusters which are not highly differentiated from neighboring areas, I would conclude there is a form of matrilateral exchange operating with either patrilineages or matrilineages. You cannot determine lineage structure from the ceramic evidence but it seems to me that only matrilateral exchange would account for three design clusters in the same site, at the same time, under circumstances where the design clusters show a general relationship to a wide area.

C : 26, 27, 28, 53
D : 26, 27, 48, 49, 51, 63, 64
E : 26, 27, 48, 50, 51, 53
F : 26, 27, 49, 51, 62, 63, 64
G : 26, 27, 51, 57, 62
H : 26, 28, 49, 58, 64
I : 26, 50, 51, 53, 57
J : 27, 28, 49, 63, 65
K : 27, 28, 62, 63, 64, 65
L : 28, 59, 63, 64
M : 28, 59, 65, 66
N : 28, 60, 62
O : 48, 63, 64, 65
P : 49, 62, 63, 65, 69
Q : 50, 59, 63, 64
R : 53, 70
S : 59, 63, 65
T : 59, 68
U : 60, 68
V : 61, 64, 65
W : 61, 65, 66
X : 62, 70
Y : 65, 66, 68
Z : 67, 68

The description of the machine coded variable numbers is to be found in Table XII.

*Location of flint-chipping areas.*—It is clear from analysis of these lithic constellations that two rather distinct bases account for their formation. Constellations A through H, and J, are representative of particular areas of the site where flint-chipping was regularly performed. Constellation A occurred principally in the areas directly southwest of the entrances to Structures I, II, and III, where primary production of bipolar cores (made on pebble cores modified from glacially derived chert nodules) was carried out.

Constellation B occurred at several areas on the site but it was generally found outside the walls of the major structures. This constellation discloses the production of block cores from unmodified chert nodules.

Constellation C occurred to the southeast of ancillary Structures $II_A$ and $II_B$. It reveals the production of bifacial blades from roughly trimmed blanks or cores.

Constellation D occurred in areas to the northeast of ancillary Structures $I_B$ and $II_B$, and in areas to the northwest of ancillary Structures $I_A$ and $II_A$. This constellation discloses areas

where the production of bipolar cores from pebble cores was carried out and where some of these bipolar cores and the derived flakes were used.

Constellation E occurred outside the east wall of Structures I, II, and III, and represents the production of bifacial blades from large bipolar cores and pebble cores.

Constellation F occurred primarily to the immediate southeast of ancillary Structure $II_B$ and represents an area where block cores were reduced to small bipolar cores some of which were utilized along with the derived flakes.

Constellation G occurred between the entrance to Structure I and the southern hearth; between the entrance to Structure II and the central hearth; to the north of the southeastern hearth, and to the south of the northwestern hearth in Structure III. This constellation represents the final trimming of bifacial blanks (some of which had functioned as blades) into corner-notched projectile points.

Constellation H occurred directly to the east of ancillary Structures $I_A$ and $II_A$ and represents areas where stemmed points and bipolar cores were produced from block cores.

Constellation J occurred just to the west of ancillary Structure $I_B$ and to the north of ancillary Structure $II_B$. This constellation probably represents areas where block cores were being reduced to produce immediately utilizable flakes.

*Faunal associations.*—The lithic Constellations I, and K through Z, do not seem to represent areas of flint-chipping. Unlike Constellation A through H, unused cores and high frequencies of unused flakes are absent. The interpretation of these remaining constellations is therefore somewhat more tentative. Two of these constellations have no lithic materials associated with them:

Constellation Y consisted entirely of mammal, fish, and turtle bone. It occurred principally in Feature 45, 20, and 40 and can probably be interpreted as the refuse from meals.

Constellation Z consisted of bird and turtle bone. It occurred outside and to the east of the entrance to Structure I, and outside and to the north of the entrance to Structure III. No bird bone were found within any of the structures on the site and these outside occurrences accounted for most of the avian fauna recovered from this component. A large number of the bird bones were uncharred and the only nonfunctional item

## TABLE XII  CORRELATION COEFFICIENT MATRIX
## MIDDLE WOODLAND COMPONENT STONE AND BONE

Machine Coded Variables

|  |  |
|---|---|
| 26: | Decortication Flakes |
| 27: | Block Flakes |
| 28: | Flat Flakes |
| 48: | Pebble Cores |
| 49: | Block Cores |
| 50: | Bipolar Cores, Unused |
| 51: | Retouch Flakes |
| 53: | Bifacial Blades |
| 57: | Notched Points |
| 58: | Stemmed Points |
| 59: | End Scrapers |
| 60: | Side Scrapers |
| 61: | Notched Scrapers |
| 62: | Bladelets |
| 63: | Utilized Flakes |
| 64: | Utilized Bipolar Cores |
| 65: | Mammal Bone |
| 66: | Fish Bone |
| 67: | Bird Bone |
| 68: | Turtle |
| 69: | Worked Bone |
| 70: | Copper Scrap |

Correlation coefficient matrix (each cell shows r and a):

| | 26 | 27 | 28 | 48 | 49 | 50 | 51 | 53 | 57 | 58 | 59 | 60 | 61 | 62 | 63 | 64 | 65 | 66 | 67 | 68 | 69 | 70 |
|---|---|---|---|---|---|---|---|---|---|---|---|---|---|---|---|---|---|---|---|---|---|---|
| 26 | 26 | | | | | | | | | | | | | | | | | | | | | |
| 27 | .925 <.01 | 27 | | | | | | | | | | | | | | | | | | | | |
| 28 | .810 <.01 | .851 <.01 | 28 | | | | | | | | | | | | | | | | | | | |
| 48 | .652 <.01 | .576 <.01 | | 48 | | | | | | | | | | | | | | | | | | |
| 49 | .552 <.01 | .531 <.01 | .622 <.01 | .296 <.05 | 49 | | | | | | | | | | | | | | | | | |
| 50 | .588 <.01 | .527 <.01 | | | .725 <.01 | 50 | | | | | | | | | | | | | | | | |
| 51 | .452 <.01 | .459 <.01 | | .481 <.01 | .290 <.01 | .531 <.01 | 51 | | | | | | | | | | | | | | | |
| 53 | .443 <.01 | .411 <.01 | .302 <.05 | .671 <.01 | | .860 <.01 | .506 <.01 | 53 | | | | | | | | | | | | | | |
| 57 | .328 <.01 | | | | | .392 <.01 | .238 <.05 | .316 <.01 | 57 | | | | | | | | | | | | | |
| 58 | .317 <.01 | | | | .369 <.01 | | .279 <.05 | | | 58 | | | | | | | | | | | | |
| 59 | | | | | .338 <.01 | | .277 <.05 | | | | 59 | | | | | | | | | | | |
| 60 | | | | | .351 <.01 | | | | | | | 60 | | | | | | | | | | |
| 61 | | | | | | | | | | | | | 61 | | | | | | | | | |
| 62 | .358 <.01 | .321 <.05 | .357 <.01 | .286 <.05 | | .288 <.05 | | .299 <.05 | | | | | .257 <.05 | 62 | | | | | | | | |
| 63 | .613 <.01 | .572 <.01 | .609 <.01 | .331 <.01 | .498 <.01 | .251 <.05 | .552 <.01 | | .280 <.05 | | | .280 | .292 <.05 | .548 <.01 | 63 | | | | | | | |
| 64 | .542 <.01 | .513 <.01 | .407 <.01 | .375 <.01 | .236 <.05 | .540 <.01 | .344 <.01 | | | .271 <.05 | .386 <.01 | | .300 <.05 | .330 <.01 | .543 <.01 | 64 | | | | | | |
| 65 | | .422 <.01 | .440 <.01 | | | .369 <.01 | | | .296 <.05 | | .275 <.05 | | .301 <.01 | .333 <.01 | .350 <.01 | .407 <.01 | 65 | | | | | |
| 66 | | | .327 <.01 | | | .369 <.01 | | | | | .268 <.05 | | .368 <.01 | | | | .507 <.01 | 66 | | | | |
| 67 | | | | | | | | | | | | | | | | .374 <.01 | .314 <.05 | | 67 | | | |
| 68 | | | | | | | | | | | | | .286 <.05 | .269 <.05 | | | | | .238 <.05 | 68 | | |
| 69 | | | .301 <.05 | | | | | | | | | | .254 <.05 | | | .300 <.05 | .436 <.01 | | .290 <.05 | | 69 | |
| 70 | | | | | | | | | .284 <.05 | | | | .298 <.05 | | | | | | | | | 70 |

of worked bone was an eagle talon. This suggests some form of ritualized food avoidance, but this explanation is only speculative.

Constellation K occurred at the eastern edge of ancillary Structure $I_B$, and just to the west of ancillary Structure $II_B$. This constellation probably represents the use and retouching of bladelets, utilized flakes, and bipolar cores in the initial preparation of the meat from mammals for drying.

Constellation M occurred to the northeast of Feature 45; to the southwest of Feature 12; to the southwest of Feature 20; and to the northeast of Feature 31, all interior hearths. This may represent the use and retouching of scrapers by women for the preparation of meals containing mammal and/or fish. It may also represent areas where hides were scraped and worked, in which case the fish bone would be present merely as the remains of previous meals prepared or consumed at those hearths. The presence of several bladelets and bone and copper awls in these areas, while not statistically significant, may add strength to an interpretation of these areas as locations where garments were prepared.

Constellation O occurred just to the north of those areas where Constellation M was noted with the exception of the area near Feature 12. It consisted of much split mammal bone, slightly worked pebble cores, heavily battered bipolar cores, and heavy utilized flakes, predominantly made on block flakes.

Just to the northwest of the latter constellation, Constellation P *always* occurred. The latter consists of blades, bladelets, gouge-end bipolar cores with transverse edge striae, and worked bone tools. These two constellations are probably best interpreted as two related areas where a male was engaged in the production of bone tools.

Constellation S occurred only along the outside west wall of Structure I, about eight feet from ancillary Structure $I_B$. It consisted of end scrapers, utilized flakes, and mammal bone and probably represents some stage in the butchering process: a different step in the butchering process than that represented by Constellation K.

Constellation V and W are also indicative of processing mammalian subsistence resources. Both, however, had a rather low level of statistical probability ($a = .05$) and may well be the result of sampling error. This is especially likely when it is made clear that both constellations are based on two occurrences of notched scrapers, thus accounting for all four of the notched scrapers recovered from this component.

Constellation V, consisting of the notched scrapers, bipolar cores, and mammal bone, occurred to the northwest of Features 45 and 20. These may be the areas where mammal bone was cleaned prior to being manufactured into artifacts.

Constellation W occurred to the east of ancillary Structure $II_A$ and the the north of ancillary Structure $III_A$. This constellation consists of notched scrapers, mammal and fish bone. It may represent a final stage in preparing these faunal resources for drying, but it may also be a result of sampling error.

Constellation T, consisting of end scrapers and turtle shell, occurred only in Structure I, to the southwest of Feature 45 and just to the right of the entrance. In this area fragments of a cut and scraped turtle plastron and carapace were also recovered in association with eight choke-cherry stones. I would interpret this as evidence that a turtle shell rattle was being made at this location.

Constellation U, consisting of side scrapers and turtle bone and shell, occurred just to the west of Feature 40 within Structure III, and along the west wall in Structure I, to the west of Feature 12. This constellation probably represents the processing of turtle meat.

*Tool kits.*—The six remaining lithic constellations do not have any associated fauna, nor are their locii of occurrence particularly significant. Their covariance at all areas of the site clearly indicates that they were used together as tool kits but, with two exceptions, their function cannot be ascertained.

Constellation N, consisting of flakes of bifacial retouch, bladelets, and side scrapers, occurred about seven feet southwest of the entrance of Structure I, II, and III. This constellation clearly represents a resharpening activity, but why this was performed only on side scrapers and bladelets is uncertain. The uniform location of this activity is also unclear. Granted that sunlight was needed to see what was being accomplished, does this location represent the end of the shadows cast by the houses themselves? If so, these activities must have been performed in the morning. Further speculation along these lines clearly leads to fantasy.

Constellation I occurred within Structures I and II along the wall opposite the entrance. It also occurred at Structure IV in the northern portion. This constellation consists of decortication and retouch flakes, bipolar cores, bifacial blades and corner-notched projectile points.

Constellation L, consisting of retouch and utilized flakes, gouge-end bipolar cores, and end scrapers, occurred just to the northwest of every interior hearth on the site.

Constellation Q, consisting of utilized and unutilized bipolar cores, utilized flakes (predominantly decortication flakes) and end scrapers, occurred along the west wall of Structure I; to the west of Feature 45; and along the east wall of Structure II to the east of Feature 20. If any interpretation can be made for these three constellations it might be that I represents a male's hunting kit, L represents a woodworking or whitling kit, a Q represents tools used in preparing vegetal foods. These interpretations are quite speculative.

A much firmer basis exists for the interpretation of Constellations R and X. The former consists of bifacial blades and copper scrap and occurred between the entrance to Structure II and Feature 39, just outside the entrance to Structure I. The latter consists of bladelets and copper scrap and occurred just to the east of the entrance outside Structures I and II. It was also in this area (although somewhat closer to Feature 39) that two bifacial choppers with crushed edges were recovered. These two constellations clearly represent two areas of copper working, but whether the differences between them indicate sequent phases in the production of copper tools or different tools employed in the manufacture of different copper artifacts is indeterminate.

*Functional relationships.*—From the above analyses, it is clear that very little evidence exists for the functional equivalence of distinct lithic tool types. To some extent there may have been free variation between the use of side and end scrapers in processing turtle shell for further use. The bifacial blades may be viewed as functionally equivalent to the bladelets in the production of copper artifacts, but these cases could be argued to represent true functional differences as much as individual preferences for particular tools in a functionally equivalent task. Of some interest is the almost complete restriction of utilized and concave-end bipolar cores to constellations associated with woodworking or processing mammals. This is consistent with their inferred use as wedges and gouges. It may also be the case that the bipolar cores were used occasionally as replacements for notched scrapers, and that they were functionally equivalent to interchange-able end scrapers and side scrapers in the process-ing of hides. These are only hypotheses, however, and larger samples are needed to test them. The lack of any evidence for functional equivalence between the stemmed points and the corner-notched points is noteworthy. Of the five stemmed points recovered from the Middle Woodland component, four were associated with structures presumed to be fish drying racks while none of the corner-notched points were associ-ated with these structures. While the bipolar cores associated with these stemmed points are not considered related to the processing of fish, this may not be true of the stemmed points. One interpretation of the functional disparity between stemmed and notched points would be that the former often were used as something other than projectile points. No evidence in the form of wear patterns supports the contention that stemmed points functioned as knives, however, and this use is merely suggested.

## SYNTHESIS

*Sociological implications.*—One striking fact about the distribution of the lithic constellations is their tendency to duplicate themselves at several similar areas of the site. Large centralized areas of uniform function do not seem to exist. If every hearth within a structure represents a nuclear family, it is clear that the adult male of each household individually performed all the phases of bone and stone tool production which can be demonstrated for the component, while the adult female individually performed all of the final food processing and skin preparation. Some activities, such as the manufacture of copper tools and the initial butchering and processing of fauna, appear to have carried out jointly by all males or all females from the extended family (represented by joint occupation of a single structure). If the unusual disposition of avian remains can be taken as evidence for some form of ceremonialism these activities appear to have been jointly performed by each of the closely related groups inhabiting the two house clusters (Structures I and II; Structures III and IV). There would seem to be no direct archaeological evidence for any form of activity that the entire community performed as a group.

The fact that sherds of Linear Incised, Interrupted variety were associated with ancillary Structures $I_A$, $I_B$, and $II_B$, and Miscellaneous Punctate sherds were associated with ancillary Structures $I_B$ and $III_A$, is evidence that the women living in the northwestern structures (Structures III and IV) made use of the drying racks associated with the southeastern house cluster. It is doubtful that these examples repre-sent the type of intra-community ceramic exchange noted for the Sio of New Guinea (Harding, *op. cit.*: 90-91) for in that case the "foreign" ceramics should also occur at the hearths within the structures. The distribution of those types noted as intra-house cluster transfers seem more directly related to the utilization of faunal (and thus subsistence) resources.

It may not be too farfetched to view the data as evidence for the collective pooling of food resources at a nuclear or extended family level, and some form of reciprocity between several such households (Sahlins, 1965: 142, 147-48). Between the two households within a single house cluster there is a "balanced reci-procity," while the intra-house clusters seem to have been practicing a type of "generalized reci-procity" with goods moving from the southeast to the northwest house cluster. The entire occupation of this component was rather short-lived, and as Sahlins (*idem*: 147) has noted, "Failure to reciprocate does not cause the giver of stuff to stop giving: the goods move one way, in favor of the have-not, for a very long period."

If the interpretation of these ceramic transfers as evidence of reciprocity is correct, it reinforces the view that kinship distance is reflected in terms of spatial distance at the site. This is what would be expected on the basis of Sahlins' model (1965: 149-55). At a sub-chiefdom level of social organization, material goods (including foodstuffs) tend to flow toward the junior or subordinate end of whatever ranking scale may exist (Sahlins, 1965: 160, 174, 200-1). The further application of this model for generalized reciprocity to the Middle Woodland component at Summer Island leads to the speculation that the leader of the group probably lived either in Structure I or Structure II.

*Sexual composition.*—Returning now to Figure 8, it may be possible to distinguish the areas within Structures I and II, which were occupied by males and females (the same pattern can be assumed to have repeated itself within Structures III and IV).[8] In general, the areas within the structures which surrounded the hearths were rather free from artifacts, post molds, or features. Along the inside of the walls the floor was easily separated into distinct functional areas, each of which indicated predominantly either male or female-oriented activity. Within Structure II a single area opposite the entrance showed evidence, in the form of the production of bone tools and in the presence of what may be a hunting tool kit, that it was probably occupied by an adult male. To the north of this lay a concentration of ceramic sherds and bone tools clearly indicating that an adult female habitually used the area. Proceeding counterclockwise, the next area to the southeast was an area which projectile points were manufactured and it possibly represented a work area for the first, and perhaps another male, probably the sub-adult son of the first. South of this was an area where clothing was manufactured. This need not represent a second adult female. It could indicate a work area where the mother and daughter of the first male were employed. From this point in the structure to the entrance, male-related activity occurred. Beside the hearth and

along the west wall was an area of female activity. The total number of people consistently working within this structure would seem to be an adult male, possibly his mother, his wife, his sub-adult son, and at least one younger son and daughter. This would give a minimum total of five or six inhabitants, a figure in close agreement with the previous estimates derived from analyses of available floor space (p. 38).

Within Structure I there seems to be some degree of bilateral symmetry observable in the arrangement of functional areas. Proceeding from the entrance along both walls there occurred areas of male-related flint-chipping activity, followed successively by female-related areas of food preparation. Along the east wall this was followed by an area of bone tool production. The next functional area along both walls seemed to clearly represent female-related hide processing, and finally, along both walls, opposite the entrance, areas where hunting tool kits occurred. This seems most likely to represent two distinct nuclear families with the adult males congregating near the rear of the lodge. Following this along the east wall was an area where several males (possibly sub-adult son and father) carried out flint-knapping activities and manufactured bone tools. To the south of this on the east wall, and directly south of the adult female area along the west wall were areas where female-related activity occurred, while within the entrance and for some distance to the north a number of males apparently slept. This final male-related area was considerably smaller along the east wall than along the west wall.

A reasonable interpretation for this distribution would be that the inhabitants of Structure I form a patrilocal extended family. The two nuclear families are arranged in parallel fashion along the long walls of the house, probably with the head of the family in the place of honor opposite the door (Densmore, *op. cit.*; Rogers, 1967: *loc. cit.*; Pilling, 1966: 242-44; Rogers, 1962: 370). The fact that the two adult males apparently were father and son may account for the two halves of the house not mirroring each other exactly, the son presumably having no sub-adult son with whom he chipped flint or manufactured bone tools. The population for this structure would thus seem to consist of the elder male, his wife and probably at least one sub-adult unmarried son and daughter, the younger

---

8. The method employed in this stage of the analysis follows the procedures Pilling (1966) outlined in his analysis of sexual composition at the Porter site VIII in central Michigan.

male, his wife and possibly several young children. This would be a total of four adults, two sub-adults, and an unknown number of children. The minimum figure based on this estimate would be eight. This is less than predicted by the figures based on analysis of floor space which estimated 10 or 11 people in a structure of this size. While the estimated minimum population of eight is quite close to the estimates Pilling arrived at for the multiple family structures at the Porter Site 8 (1966: 241-42), a larger number of young children would raise the Summer Island figures to those obtained by the previous estimates based on the methodology employed by Cook and Heizer (1965). In any event, both methods indicate that the population for the entire community was between 25 and 35, thus lying within, but on the low end of the population range for a patrilocal band (Service, 1962: 70; Owen, 1965: 675-85).

# 8. Conclusions

The foregoing analyses have disclosed the nature of the Middle Woodland occupation of Summer Island. The community consisted of about 30 individuals, representing two extended families and two nuclear families, occupying four structures. Analysis of the areal distribution of various types of artifacts leads to the inference that the preferred residence pattern was for patrilocality and that band exogamy and some form of cross-cousin marriage were practiced. Social organization does not seem to have reached any level beyond that of the patrilocal band. While one family apparently contained the leader of the band who provided for the less successful families, there is no indication that this was due to ascribed status. It may merely have been due to his seniority.

On a more concrete level, these analyses have demonstrated that the basic economic unit in terms of subsistence activity was the patrilocal extended family household although the individual nuclear families appear to have been quite independent in the manufacture and processing of non-foodstuffs. While enterprises such as net fishing during the spawning runs may have involved the cooperation of the entire band, no archaeological evidence was recovered which would support this hypothesis.

The site was occupied from about the first spring thaw to the late summer. The major subsistence resource during the early part of this occupation, and indeed probably the principal reason for it, was the sturgeon which were netted or speared as they spawned in the shallow water along the rocky shoals surrounding the island.

Small mammals, possibly an occasional moose or deer, the results of miscellaneous hook-and-line and spear-fishing, and turtle added to the dried sturgeon probably supplied a great part of the diet through the mid-summer. To this can probably be added many of the locally available plants (see Yarnell, *op. cit.*: 54-61). In the late summer and early autumn, large mammals such as deer and bear, supplemented by the available plant foods (*idem*: p. 61-73), were utilized. The site apparently was abandoned before the local spawning runs of lake trout and whitefish in October. This is assumed to indicate a reliance on some nonlocal resource then available. Wild rice is a good candidate. Analysis of the strata and structures quite difinitely indicated that the site was not occupied for more than three or four seasons. No reason for its abandonment was apparent.

While faunal resources may have been difficult to obtain no such limitations seem to have been imposed upon the lithic materials. Vast amounts of chert debitage attest the easy availability of this stone. Although generally of low quality, its great abundance made the search for more easily controlled material unnecessary. The amounts of scrap copper recovered, often as sizeable pieces, may indicate that a feeling of affluence prevailed here as well. This is in marked contrast to those sites in Ontario where similar artifact styles occur at the same general time period. James Wright characterizes the Ontario Laurel components as small sites which

> rarely produce deposits that can be profitably excavated . . . Subsurface features are rare

and they generally consist of simple fire-stone concentrations interpreted as hearths. What little subsistence data are available suggests an economy centered on the hunting of moose and beaver, although regional and seasonal factors could play havoc with such a general observation, based as it is on very limited information. A characteristic that is difficult to qualify is the nature of the cultural debris itself. Large flakes, bone fragments artifacts and artifact fragments are rare in contrast to the preceeding Archaic and following Late Woodland assembledges. Very small tools are abundant and the lithic and bone refuse have generally been reduced to minute fragments. In short, there appears to have been an extensive utilization of the raw materials with very little wastage . . . This situation is quite contrary to that noted in the east with reference to the Point Peninsula and Saugeen foci, [1967: 94].

While no data are given on the size of bone fragments or debitage, none of the finished artifacts are significantly smaller than their counterparts in the North Bay, Point Peninsula or Minnesota Laurel components. Nor are they noticeably smaller than their functional equivalents from Summer Island. With the exception of Heron Bay, all of Wright's Ontario Laurel sites are poor indeed by comparison to Summer Island. While the Pelican Falls site may have as many as 20 vessels represented, only two others have more than five (J. Wright: 1967 *passim*). These sites are all quite small. Most excavated sites show a rather high frequency of projectile points and scrapers. Taken with Wright's characterization of the faunal remains, these small sites may be interpreted as short-term fall and winter hunting camps occupied by a single family. The intensive utilization of raw materials at these sites may simply be a factor of temporarily limited access to the sources.

To some extent, however, even the large sites such as Heron Bay and Pelican Falls (which probably represent multi-family summer and early fall fishing stations) seem to show a greater utilization of lithic material than the functionally equivalent Summer Island site. One explanation for this may be found in the relatively large

numbers of scrapers which occur at the Ontario sites, thus adding to the percentage of flaked stone showing evidence of deliberate work (Wright, 1967: 32, 64, 68). This is also the situation at the Naomikong Point site where over 1100 scrapers were recovered (Janzen, 1968). From these sites the frequency of bipolar cores is correspondingly low while at Summer Island some evidence for the functional equivalence of bipolar cores and scrapers has been suggested. Again, the bipolar core technique does not seem to have been of much importance in the North Bay components at the Mero or at the Porte des Morts site (Mason, 1966; 1967).

Mason (1967: 333-34, 338-43) noted the regional diversity that characterized the lithic and copper industries of these Northern Tier Middle Woodland cultures, and added, "What is most distinctive of the Anderson-Nutimik-Laurel-(North Bay)-Saugeen-Point Peninsula continuum is of course the pottery." This situation has also been remarked upon by James Wright: "Not only are many of the ceramic attributes unique to the [Laurel] tradition, but a substantial number exhibit a homogeneity which is quite surprising when one considers the extensive area involved," (1967: 93). Taken in conjunction with the variations noted in lithic and copper working (*idem*: p. 127-29), this leads Wright to see a movement of people into the area from the northwest. In the discussion of ceramics (Brose, n.d.b), the author rejects this interpretation in favor of viewing the ceramic continuum, albeit poorly understood, as a regional adoption of ceramic styles originated in the Illinois area. If the social structure deduced to have existed at Summer Island can be imputed to similar sites throughout the Middle Woodland Lake Forest, a processual explanation is available to account for widespread homogeneity and regionally distinctive lithic traditions.

In his discussion of the composition of patrilocal bands, Owen (1965: 678) indicates that the diversity between male and female "culture" could reach the point where, while all adult males were native speakers of one language some of the adult females were native speakers of different languages or dialects. Owen explains this as a result of band exogamy and low population density which, "will inevitably lead to selection of mates from some distance, often fifty miles away or more" (1965: 683). The results of such a diffustion of females with their attendant cultural background would soon lead to the standardization of a ceramic design repetoires over large geographical areas while leaving realtively stable male-related lithic industires to develop along more local lines. Such a movement of females would not lead to a total loss of ceramic attribute clusters (unless a totally random mating pattern were concomittant with patrilocal residence) anymore than the lack of male movement would lead to unvarying and totally isolated lithic attribute clusters. It would, however, account for the widespread occurrence of quite similar ceramic modes such as are observed.

To carry these speculations further, some of these ceramic modes, while geographically widespread relative to much of the male-related artifact types, still show definite limits not all of which coincide. Granted the high degree of mobility which the economic pattern imposes upon these central-based wandering communities (Beardsley, *et al.*, 1955: 138-40), it would not be difficult to see ceramic styles diffuse quite rapidly (say within several generations) from one end of the Lake Forest to the other. If this had in fact occurred, and if ceramic styles ultimately derived from Illinois once entered such a system at either (or both) ends, the archaeological picture may well present the impression of a sweeping occupation of the central area by a cohesive culture which bears little relationship to the preceeding Archaic occupations. This would be especially true if the economic patterns of that central area, in response to changing environmental conditions, were under-going a readaptation towards a more diffuse economy with the intendant replacement of many of the older types of functional tools and the addition of several new ones (see Cleland, 1966: 42-45). The only movement of people this speculative model would require is the seasonal movement of exogamous patrilocal bands utilizing the available resources of the Lake Forest Formation, and the post-nuptial movement of women between bands within the area.

# References

Ayers, J., D. Chandler, G. Lauff, C. Powers, and E. Henson
 1958 Currents and Water Masses of Lake Michigan. *Great Lakes Research Institute of the University of Michigan,* Publication No. 3. Ann Arbor.

Beardsley, R., P. Holder, A. Krieger, B. Meggers, J. Rinaldo, and P. Kutsche
 1955 Functional and Evolutionary Implications of Community Patterning. In "Seminars in Archaeology: 1955," *Memoirs of the Society for American Anthroplogy,* No. 11 pp. 129-57. Salt Lake City.

Binford, Lewis R. and George I. Quimby
 1963 Indian Sites and Chipped Stone Materials in the Northern Lake Michigan Area. *Fieldiana: Anthropology,* Vol. 36, No. 12, pp. 277-307. Chicago.

Blair, Emma
 1911 *Indian Tribes of the Upper Mississippi Valley and Great Lakes.* Vol. I. C. Thomas, Cleveland.

Blalock, Hubert M., Jr.
 1960 *Social Statistics.* McGraw-Hill Inc., New York.

Brose, David S.
 n.d.a Geological Analysis of Beach and Dune Sands in Northern Lake Michigan. *The Ohio Journal of Science.* In press.
 n.d.b. The Archaeology of Summer Island: Changing Settlement Systems in Northern Lake Michigan. *Anthropological Papers, Museum of Anthropology, University of Michigan,* No. 41. Ann Arbor.

Bunzel, Ruth (editor)
 1929 The Pueblo Potter. *Columbia University, Contributions to Anthropology,* No. 8. New York.

Burlington, Richard S.
 1956 *Handbook of Mathematical Tables and Formulas.* Handbook Publishers Inc., Sandusky.

Burt, William H.
 1954 *The Mammals of Michigan.* University of Michigan Press, Ann Arbor.

Burt, William H. and Richard P. Grossenheider
 1956 *A Field Guide to the Mammals.* The Riverside Press, Cambridge.

Callender, Charles
 1962 Social Organization of the Central Algonkian. *Papers of the Public Museum of Milwaukee,* No. 7 Milwaukee.

Cleland, Charles E.
 1966 The Prehistoric Animal Ecology and Ethnozoology of the Upper Great Lakes Region. *Anthropological Papers, Museum of Anthropology, University of Michigan,* No. 29. Ann Arbor.

Cleland, Charles E. and G. Richard Peske
    1968    The Spider Cave Site. *Anthropological Papers, Museum of Anthropology, University of Michigan,* No. 33, pp. 20-60. Ann Arbor.
Cook, S.F. and Robert F. Heizer
    1965    The Quantitative Approach to the Relation Between Population and Settlement Size. *Report, University of California Archaeological Survey* No. 64, Berkeley.
Cushing, Edward J.
    1965    Problems in the Quarternary Phytogeography of the Great Lakes Region. In: *The Quarternary of the United States,* edited by D. Frey and H. Wright, pp. 403-16. Princeton University Press. Princeton.
Dailey, R. C. and J. V. Wright
    1955    The Malcolm Site. *Transactions of the Royal Canadian Institute,* Vol. 31, Part I, pp. 24-69. Toronto.
Deetz, James
    1965    The Dynamics of Stylistic Change in Arikara Ceramics. *Illinois Studies in Anthropology,* No. 4. University of Illinois Press, Urbana.
Densmore, Francis
    1929    Chippewa Customs. *Bureau of American Ethnology Bulletin* 86. Washington, D.C.
Dice, Lee R.
    1938    The Canadian Biotic Province with Special Reference to the Mammals. *Ecology,* Vol. 19, No. 4, pp. 503-14. Urbana.
Eggan, Fred
    1966    *The American Indian.* Aldine, Chicago.
Emerson, J.N.
    1955    The Kant Site: A Point Peninsula Manifestation in Renfrew County, Oniario. *Transactions of the Royal Canadian Institute,* Vol. 31, Part 1, pp. 3-23. Toronto.
Fitting, James E.
    1968a   The Spring Creek Site. *Anthropological Papers, Museum of Anthropology, University of Michigan,* No. 32, pp. 1-78. Ann Arbor.
    1968b   Northern Lake Michigan Lithic Industries. *Anthropological Papers, Museum of Anthropology, University of Michigan,* No. 33, pp. 116-133. Ann Arbor.
    n.d.    The Schultz Site at Green Point: A Stratified Occupation Area in the Saginaw Valley of Michigan. *Memoirs of the Museum of Anthropology, University of Michigan,* No. 4. In Press.
Fitting, James E., Jerry DeVisscher, and Edward J. Wahla
    1966    The Paleo-Indian Occupation of the Holcombe Beach. *Anthropological Papers, Museum of Anthropology, University of Michigan,* No. 27. Ann Arbor.
Fitting, James E., David S. Brose, Henry T. Wright and James Dinerstein
    1969    The Goodwin-Gresham Site, 20 IS 8, Iosco County, Michigan. *The Wisconsin Archeologist,* Vol. 50, No. 3, pp. 125-83. Lake Mills.
Freeman, Leslie G., Jr. and James A. Brown
    1964    Statistical Analysis of Carter Ranch Pottery. *Fieldiana: Anthropology,* Vol. 55, pp. 126-54. Chicago.
Griffin, James B.
    1952    Some Early and Middle Woodland Pottery Types in Illinois. *Illinois State Museum Science Papers,* Vol. 5, pp. 93-129. Springfield.
    1965    Ceramic Complexity and Cultural Development: The Eastern United States as a Case Study. In "Ceramics and Man" edited by Fredrick R. Matson, *Viking Fund Publications in Anthropology,* No. 41, pp. 104-13. New York.
Grigor'ev, G.P.
    1967    A New Reconstruction of Above Ground Dwelling of Kostenki I. *Current Anthropology,* Vol. 8, No. 4, pp. 344-49. Chicago.

Hawkins, Arthur S.
1964    The Mississippi Flyway. *Waterfowl Tommorrow,* pp. 185-207, United States Department of Interior. Washington, D.C.

Harding, Thomas
1967    *Voyagers of the Vitiaz Strait, A Study of a New Guinea Trade System.* University of Washington, Seattle.

Hickerson, Harold
1960    The Feast of the Dead Among the Seventeenth Century Algonkians of the Upper Great Lakes. *American Anthropologist,* Vol. 62, No. 1, pp. 81-107. Menasha.
1962    The Southwestern Chippewa. *American Anthropological Association Memoir,* No. 92. Menasha.
1967    Some Implications of the Theory of Particularity, or "Atomist" of Northern Algonkians. *Current Anthropology,* Vol. 8, No. 4, pp. 313-44. Chicago.

Hilger, Sister M. Inez
1951    Chippewa Child Life and Its Cultural Background. Bureau of *American Ethnology,* Bulletin 146. Washington, D.C.

Hockett, Charles
1964    Proto-Central Algonkian Kinship. In *Exploration in Cultural Anthropology,* edited by W. Goodenough, pp. 762-89. Columbia University Press, New York.

Hubbs, Carl and Karl Lagler
1961    *The Fish of the Great Lakes Region.* University of Michigan Press, Ann Arbor.

Janzen, Donald
1968    Naomikong Point and the Dimensions of Laurel in the Lake Superior Region. *Anthropological Papers, Museum of Anthropology, University of Michigan*, No. 36. Ann Arbor.

Johnson, Eldon
1969    Archaeological Evidence for Wild Rice Use. *Science,* Vol. 169, pp. 276-77. Lancaster.

Johnston, Richard B.
1968    The Archaeology of the Serpent Mounds Site. *Royal Ontario Museum Art and Archaeology Occasional Paper,* No. 10. Toronto.

Kinietz, Vernon
1940    The Indians of the Western Great Lakes. *Occasional Contributions from the Museum of Anthropology, University of Michigan,* No. 10. Ann Arbor.

Kuchler, A.W.
1964    Potential Natural Vegetation of the Conterminous United States. *American Geographical Society, Special Publications,* No. 36. New York.

Longacre, William A.
1964    Sociological Implications of the Ceramic Analyses. *Fieldiana: Anthropology,* Vol. 55, pp. 155-70. Chicago.

MacNeish, Richard S.
1958    An Introduction to the Archaeology of Southeast Manitoba. *National Museum of Canada Bulletin* No. 157. Ottawa.

McPherron, Alan L.
1967    The Juntunen Site and the Late Woodland Prehistory of the Upper Great Lakes Area. *Anthropological Papers, Museum of Antrhopology, University of Michigan,* No. 30, Ann Arbor.

Mason, Ronald J.
1966    Two Stratified Sites on the Door Peninsula, Wisconsin. *Anthropological Papers, Museum of Anthropology, University of Michigan,* No. 26, Ann Arbor.
1967    The North Bay Component at the Porte Des Morts Site. *The Wisconsin Archeologist,* Vol. 48, No. 4, pp. 267-334. Lake Mills.

Morgan, Lewis H.
   1852    *The League of the Ho-De-No-San-Nee, or Iroquois.* Sage and Broa, Rochester.
   1881    Houses and House Life of the American Aborigines. *United States Geological Survey, Contributions to North American Ethnology,* Vol. 4. Washington, D.C.
Munsell
   1954    *Munsell Soil Color Charts.* Munsell Color Co., Inc. Baltimore.
Murdock, George P.
   1949    *Social Structure.* The Free Press. New York.
Odum, Eugene P.
   1959    *Fundamentals of Ecology.* W.B. Saunders Co. New York.
Owen, Roger C.
   1965    The Patrilocal Band: A Linguistically and Culturally Hybrid Social Unit. *American Anthropologist,* Vol. 67, No. 5, pp. 675-90. Menasha.
Peterson, Roger T.
   1963    *A Field Guide to the Birds of the Eastern United States.* The Riverside Press, Cambridge.
Pilling, Arnold R.
   1966    Life at Porter Site 8, Midland County, Michigan. *The Michigan Archaeologist,* Vol. 12, No. 4, pp. 235-48. Ann Arbor.
Prahl, Earl J. and David S. Brose
   n.d.    "The Ekdahl-Goudreau Site." Notes on file at The University of Toledo.
Ouimby, George I.
   1966    *Indian Culture and European Trade Goods.* University of Wisconsin Press, Madison.
Ritchie, William A.
   1949    An Archaeological Survey of the Trent Waterway in Ontario, Canada and Its Significance for New York State Prehistory. *Rochester Museum of Arts and Sciences Research Records,* No. 9. Rochester.
   1965    *The Archaeology of New York State.* Natural History Press. New York.
Ritchie, William A. and Richard S. MacNeish
   1949    The Pre-Iroquoian Pottery of New State. *American Antiquity,* Vol. 15, No. 2, pp. 97-124. Menasha.
Rogers, Edward S.
   1962    The Round Lake Ojibwa. *Royal Ontario Museum Art and Archaeology Occasional Paper,* No. 5. Toronto.
   1967    The Material Culture of the Mestossini. *National Museum of Canada Bulletin* No. 218. Ottawa.
Rostlund, Erhard
   1952    Freshwater Fish and Fishing in Native North America. *University of California, Geographical Publications,* No. 9. Berkeley.
Rouse, Irving
   1939    Prehistory in Haiti: A Study in Method. *Yale University Publications in Anthropology,* No. 21. New Haven.
Sahlins, Marshall D.
   1965    On the Sociology of Primitive Exchange. *The Relevance of Models for Social Anthropology.* Association of Social Anthropologists Monograph No. 1, pp. 139-236. Praeger, New York.
   1968    *Tribesmen.* Prentice-Hall. Englewood Cliffs.
Schoolcraft, Henry R.
   1851    *Personal Memoirs of a Residence of Thirty Years with the Indian Tribes on the American Frontier.* Philadelphia.
Scott, W.B.
   1954    *Freshwater Fishes of Eastern Canada.* University of Toronto.

Semenov, S.A.
1964    *Prehistoric Technology.* Barnes and Noble, New York City.

Service, Elman R.
1962    *Primitive Social Organization.* Random House, New York.

Soil Survey Manual
1962    *United States Department of Agriculture Handbook,* No. 18. Third Edition. Washington, D.C.

Speck, Frank G.
1947    *Eastern Algonkian Block-Stamp Decoration.* Archaeological Society of New Jersey. Trenton.
1948    The Iroquois. *Cranbook Museum of Science, Bulletin* No. 4. Bloomfield Hills.

Stoltman, James B.
1962    A Proposed Method for Systematizing the Modal Analysis of Pottery and Its Application to the Laurel Focus. Unpublished M.A. Thesis, University of Minnesota.

Thwaites, Ruben G., Editor
1959    *The Jesuit Relations and Allied Documents,* 1610-1791. 73 Vols. Burroughs Bros. New New City.

Titiev, Mescha
1943    The Influence of Common Residence on the Unilateral Classification of Kindred. *American Anthropologist,* Vol. 45, No. 4, pp. 511-30. Menasha.

Voegelin, E.W. and C.F. Voegelin
1946    Linguistic Considerations in Northeastern North America, In "Man in Northeastern North America," edited by Fredrick Johnson. *Papers of The Robert S. Peabody Foundation in Archaeology,* Vol. 3, pp. 127-60. Andover.

Waterman, T.T.
1925    North American Indian Dwellings. *Annual Report of the Smithsonian Institution,* 1924, pp. 461-85. Washington, D.C.

White, Anta M., Binford, Lewis R., and Mark L. Papworth
1963    Miscellaneous Studies in Typology and Classification. *Anthropological Papers, Museum of Anthropology, University of Michigan,* No. 19. Ann Arbor.
        Wilford, Lloyd A.

Wilford, Lloyd A.
1950    The Prehistoric Indians of Minnesota: Some Mounds of the Rainy River Aspect. *Minesota History,* Vol. 31, No. 3, pp. 161-71. St. Paul.
1955    A Revised Classification of the Prehistoric Cultures of Minnesota. *American Antiquity,* Vol. 21, No. 2, pp. 130-42. Salt Lake City.

Wright, Gary A.
1967    Some Aspects of Early and Mid-17th Century Exchange Networks in the Western Great Lakes. *The Michigan Archaeologist,* Vol. 13, No. 4, pp. 181-97. Ann Arbor.

Wright, James V.
1967    The Laurel Tradition and The Middle Woodland Period. *National Museum of Canada Bulletin,* No. 217. Ottawa.

Wright, James V. and James E. Anderson
1963    The Donaldson Site. *National Museum of Canada Bulletin,* No. 184. Ottawa.

Yarnell, Richard A.
1964    Aboriginal Relationships between Culture and Plant Life in the Upper Great Lakes Region. *Anthropological Papers, Museum of Anthropology, University of Michigan,* No. 23. Ann Arbor.